Jon's Chopsticks

Rebecca Milner

Level 3
(1600-word)

IBC パブリッシング

はじめに

　ラダーシリーズは、「はしご (ladder)」を使って一歩一歩上を目指すように、学習者の実力に合わせ、無理なくステップアップできるよう開発された英文リーダーのシリーズです。

　リーディング力をつけるためには、繰り返したくさん読むこと、いわゆる「多読」がもっとも効果的な学習法であると言われています。多読では、「1. 速く 2. 訳さず英語のまま 3. なるべく辞書を使わず」に読むことが大切です。スピードを計るなど、速く読むよう心がけましょう（たとえば TOEIC® テストの音声スピードはおよそ1分間に150語です）。そして1語ずつ訳すのではなく、英語を英語のまま理解するくせをつけるようにします。こうして読み続けるうちに語感がついてきて、だんだんと英語が理解できるようになるのです。まずは、ラダーシリーズの中からあなたのレベルに合った本を選び、少しずつ英文に慣れ親しんでください。たくさんの本を手にとるうちに、英文書がすらすら読めるようになってくるはずです。

《本シリーズの特徴》

- 中学校レベルから中級者レベルまで5段階に分かれています。自分に合ったレベルからスタートしてください。
- クラシックから現代文学、ノンフィクション、ビジネスと幅広いジャンルを扱っています。あなたの興味に合わせてタイトルを選べます。
- 巻末のワードリストで、いつでもどこでも単語の意味を確認できます。レベル1、2では、文中の全ての単語が、レベル3以上は中学校レベル外の単語が掲載されています。
- カバーにヘッドホーンマークのついているタイトルは、オーディオ・サポートがあります。ウェブから購入／ダウンロードし、リスニング教材としても併用できます。

《使用語彙について》

レベル1：中学校で学習する単語約1000語

レベル2：レベル1の単語＋使用頻度の高い単語約300語

レベル3：レベル1の単語＋使用頻度の高い単語約600語

レベル4：レベル1の単語＋使用頻度の高い単語約1000語

レベル5：語彙制限なし

Contents

1. Raymond's Bowl 1
2. Getting Along 11
3. Speak Up! 23
4. What Are You Calling Me? 31
5. Safety First 39
6. Making Friends 47
7. Opposites Attract 57
8. A Quiet Place 65
9. City Life 73
10. Closing Doors 83

Word List 90

1. Raymond's Bowl
レイモンドのお椀

日本滞在10年で、シオリと結婚したイギリス人のレイモンド。10年にわたる日本生活でかなり日本の文化も習慣もわかっているつもりだった。

ある日、シオリの実家に行ったときのこと——夕食の時、義母が「はい、これがレイモンドのお茶碗、これがレイモンドのお箸……」と言って、専用の食器を渡されてびっくり。何でこんなことするんだ、とレイモンドは理由がわからない。まさか自分が外国人だから食器をシェアするのは嫌なのか？？

翌朝、そのことを忘れていたレイモンドは、まちがってシオリのお父さん用の食器を手に取ってしまった！

3. Speak Up!
自由に話そうよ！

日本人の生徒の何が不満かって聞かれたら、日本で英語を教える外国人教師のほとんどがこう答えると思う。「日本人の生徒は間違いを犯すのを恐れすぎている」。来日当初こそ、黙っている日本人学生を可愛いと思ったクリスも、あまりにもダンマリ↗

Summary

2. Getting Along
何とかやっていこう

日本に住み始めて以来、耳にタコができるほど繰り返された4つの質問——「どこから来たの？」「日本にどのくらいいるの？」「どうして日本に来たの？」、そして「いつ自分の国に帰るの？」これに最近ではもうひとつ加わった。「日本にはもう慣れた？」この質問にどうやって答えればいいのか悩むアシュレイ。滞在が長くなればなるほど、日本の暮らしには新しいルールがあることを知り、慣れたと思うと、また次のルールがあることを知るのだから……。

4. What Are You Calling Me?
私のこと何って呼んだ？

リアは顔が小さいことから、子供のころから「pin head」と呼ばれていた。アメリカでは「顔が小さい」イコール「脳も小さい」ということで褒め言葉ではない。その上、大きな目を「昆虫眼」、細い足を「チキン足」と言われ、コンプレックスのかたまりだった。そして日本で働き始めたその日、同僚になる人から、「顔、小さいわねぇ」と言われ大ショック。またか。何と答えればいい？「そうなんです」「ありがとう」「あなたもね」……。 ところがその数か月後、リアはモデルエージェントからスカウトされ、日本でモデルの仕事をやることになったのだ。

を決め込む生徒を見ていると、今では自分の教師としての能力に自信がなくなった。日本人は、外国人が間違った日本語を使ってもとても寛容なのに、なんで自分たちは完璧な英語を話そうとするんだ?! わかんないよ。

5. Safety First
安全第一

スターバックスでノートパソコンを置いたまま、コーヒーをオーダーに行くなんてカナダじゃ考えられない。でも日本なら平気なんだ。そのままトイレに行ったって、コンピュータはちゃんと残っている。日本の広告会社で働くギャビンは日本が安全なことに驚きを隠せない。タバコを忘れても、取っておいてくれるファミリーレストランがあると友達から聞いた。従業員が吸ってしまわないのか？ そこでギャビンは思った。「日本人は本当にそんなに正直なのか？ 試してやろう」

6. Making Friends
友達をつくる

イギリス人の父、日本人の母を持つソフィアだが、イギリス育ちのため日本語はまったくダメ。そこで日本で勉強を始める決心をした。まずは東京にある有名女子大に留学し、寮に入った。異文化に直面しながら、がんばりやのソフィアは何とか大学生活を乗り越える。そんなソフィアも日本に来て10年が経った。今では得意の歌で生計を立て、テレビのコマーシャルソングなども歌っている。日本文化にも慣れ、友人もできたソフィアだが、それでもまだ日本人に対してイラっとすることがあるという。それは、何か難しいことに直面したときの「どうしようもない」というあきらめの態度だそうだ。

8. A Quiet Place
どこへ行っても静かな日本

ベンは体は大きいが、恥ずかしがり屋でおとなしいアメリカ人だ。そんなベンはとにかく日本がお気に入り。アメリカは話すことがすべての社会。家族で夕食のときも、友達とバーに行っても、パーティに行っても、とにかくしゃべらないと話にならない。

Summary

7. Opposites Attract
所変われば魅力も変わる

日本文化に興味のあるジョアンナと、アメリカ文化にあこがれるハナコ。二人ともクラブで踊るのが大好きな20代女性だ。2人には共通の目的があった。ジョアンナは日本人、ハナコはアメリカ人のボーイフレンドを見つけるということ。ところがハナコは、ほかの日本人の女の子と同様、白人、金髪、たいていは痩せていて、ベビーフェースの男ばかりがお気に入り。ジョアンナにすれば、アメリカに戻ったら女性には見向きもされない男ばかりを、日本人は好きになる。ハナコもまた疑問に思っていた。なんでアメリカ人の男たちは、日本人からすると大してきれいでもない女の子とばかりつき合うのだろう??

9. City LIfe
シティライフ

ニューヨークからやってきたケーシー。東京はニューヨークに似ているところも多く、その上、バーやレストランに一人で行っても安全だし、その住み易さに満足していた。退屈な英語教師の仕事から、ニューヨーク時代の出版社勤めの経験を活かせる翻訳編集の仕事に転職もできたし、言うことなしだった。そのケーシー、東京以外の日本の地方へ行ってみることにした。すると、何だか勝手が違う。アレレレ？ ケーシーの家族が日本にやってきて、地方をドライブした時もなんだか?? そんな田舎の経験をしたケーシーの結論は、やっぱり東京がいい。

だまっていると、「どうしたんだ」「なにか意見はないのか」と矢継ぎ早に質問される。そこへいくと、日本はいい。静かにしていても誰も文句は言わないし、デートでもカウンターで並んで座れば、じっと料理人を見ているだけで話さなくても平気だし。静かな場所があちこちにある日本は最高だ！

10. Closing Doors
親切でない日本人？

世界中の人が日本人は親切で礼儀正しいという。道を聞くと教えてくれるだけでなく、わざわざ連れて行ってくれるし、わからないときは謝ってくれる。外国人は心の底から、日本人は親切だと思っているのだ。その外国人の顔にいきなりドアがガツンと当たれば、それは驚くよ——アメリカ人のデーヴは言う。デーヴいわく、日本に来た外国人なら一度はドアに顔をぶつけた経験があるという。こんなに親切な日本人がなんで次の人のためにドアを開けておいてくれないんだ!?

1. Raymond's Bowl

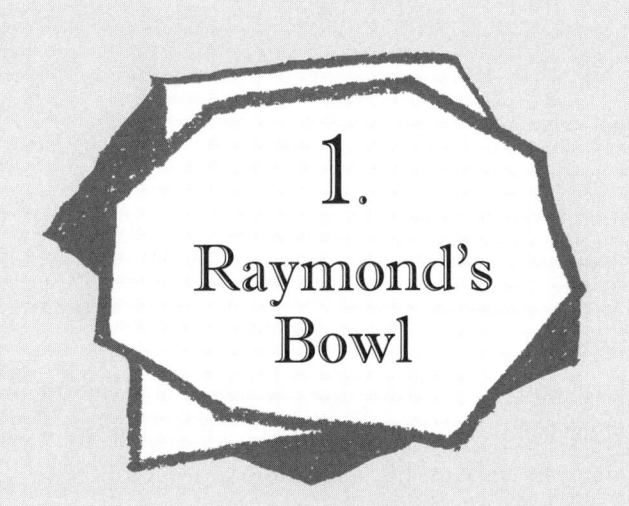

Raymond had been living in Japan for almost ten years when he married Shiori.

Raymond was from England. He studied business and Japanese in university. He also spent a year abroad studying in Kyushu. After he graduated from university, he decided to return to Japan to work on his Japanese. He got a job as an English teacher. After a year, he planned to return to England. But he never did!

Raymond discovered that he enjoyed teaching English. He was interested in language and culture, so it was a good match. Also, the short working hours left him plenty of time to study Japanese. He spent his holidays traveling around Japan and other Asian countries. Sometimes he would take many months off, traveling slowly through countries like India.

In short, Raymond lived a happy life. He heard from his friends in England about their stressful

1. RAYMOND'S BOWL

jobs. This made him grateful that he had chosen to come to Japan. His salary was okay. It was more than enough to live on. But more importantly, Raymond had time to enjoy life.

The only thing missing from his life was the perfect woman. Raymond dated many women in Japan. However, just when Raymond would get serious with a girlfriend, she would ask him to quit his free-spirited ways. His girlfriends always eventually wanted him to stop traveling, get a well-paying office job, and settle down. With his business background and Japanese skills, surely he could find a job in a bank or a trading company! This depressed Raymond. He didn't want to work in a bank or a trading company. Then he would do nothing but work!

Raymond wanted to find a woman who would enjoy traveling with him. He wanted to find a woman who really appreciated living, not just making a living.

Then Raymond met Shiori. Raymond had just returned from a long holiday in Indonesia. He started working at a new school. Shiori worked in the office at the new school.

Shiori was from Saitama. But instead of living with her parents, Shiori lived on her own in Tokyo. "My freedom is important than the money I'd save living with my parents," said Shiori. This impressed Raymond.

He thought it was strange that Japanese women lived with their parents. Western women (and men) lived on their own once they finished school. In your twenties to live with your parents was embarrassing. To be thirty and living with your parents was unthinkable!

Soon Raymond and Shiori became good friends. It was summer time then, and they enjoyed going

1. Raymond's Bowl

to fireworks and traditional Japanese festivals together. Two years later, Raymond and Shiori decided to quit their jobs and take a long trip together. They had saved enough money to travel for six months. They traveled around Australia, New Zealand, Indonesia, and Malaysia. It was on a beach in Malaysia that they realized they were in love.

Raymond loved many things about Shiori. One of the things was that Shiori never wore any make-up. All of the other Japanese women Raymond had dated wore heavy make-up. This always made him nervous. He would get used to how his girlfriend looked with make-up on. Then he would have to get used to a completely different face when she took her make-up off.

One woman Raymond dated never let him see her without make-up. Once, Raymond caught her sneaking out of bed very early in the morning to put on more make-up. But it was still dark in the room, so Raymond couldn't see her natural face. This woman made Raymond sad. They had been dating for many months. He felt that she didn't trust him enough to show him her natural face. This made Raymond worry that she wasn't showing him her natural personality, either. Soon, Raymond broke up with her.

However, with Shiori, he felt very comfortable. He could trust her completely. In fact, Raymond and Shiori often forgot that they were from two completely different cultures. Raymond wasn't English to Shiori; he was just Raymond. Shiori wasn't Japanese to Raymond; she was just Shiori.

Then they got married. Then Raymond had to meet Shiori's family. That's when he remembered that Shiori was Japanese. Shiori had free-spirited ways like Raymond, but her family was much more traditional.

Raymond and Shiori spent a week with Shiori's parents in Saitama. Raymond had had Japanese roommates before, but he had never stayed with a Japanese family. Fortunately, Raymond spoke fluent Japanese. And after living in Japan for a decade, he understood Japanese culture pretty well. Still, there was plenty of room for silly mistakes.

When Raymond sat down to dinner with Shiori's family, his mother-in-law made a presentation to Raymond about his tableware. "This is Raymond's bowl," she said to him. "These are Raymond's chopsticks. This is Raymond's tea cup."

Raymond was very confused. Was the family so afraid of him that they didn't want to share chopsticks with him? Had his mother-in-law bought new bowls and cups just for him so that he wouldn't contaminate the ones the family used?

He looked to Shiori for support. But Shiori didn't seem to notice anything unusual. So Raymond just smiled and said, "Thank you," even though he certainly didn't feel like smiling and saying "thank you!" But other than that, the first dinner went very well. Shiori's family was very polite to Raymond, and Raymond was very polite to them. They asked him many questions about England. Shiori's dad got a little drunk and was soon fast asleep at the table.

The next morning, Raymond and Shiori came downstairs for breakfast. Raymond went to the cupboard and took a bowl. Raymond saw his mother-in-law freeze. Her face looked like she was in pain. Raymond looked at the bowl in his hand. He realized that it wasn't "his bowl." Without thinking, he had taken the first bowl he'd seen in the cupboard—just like he would have done in England.

In the West, there are no different bowls for different people. All the knives and forks look the same.

Raymond remembered that "his bowl" looked slightly different, but he couldn't remember which one it was. "Does it really matter that much?" he thought. He decided to just use the bowl he had in his hands. After all, he'd already touched it.

Shiori looked at her mother and looked at Raymond, with the bowl in his hand. "Oh, Raymond is Dad today!" Shiori said laughing. Raymond

1. Raymond's Bowl

realized that all of the family members had their own bowls—not just him. This made him relieved. Surely if it were such a big deal to use the wrong bowl, she would have corrected him!

So Raymond started to put rice in the bowl. He looked at his mother-in-law to see if she had relaxed. But instead her face looked even more pained! Raymond didn't know what to do. Now what was the problem? Should he put the rice back in the rice maker, wash the bowl, and put it back in the cupboard? Maybe he should just give up and go back to bed!

Then his mother-in-law asked shyly: "Are you going to put miso soup in with the rice?"
Not only had Raymond taken the father's bowl, but he was putting rice in the bowl for miso soup! When Raymond realized his "double mistake," he had to laugh. He put down the bowl and threw up his hands. "It's all too complicated!" he said. "How can I remember which bowl is for which food? And which bowl belongs to which person?" Later, he asked his wife: "Why didn't you help me?"

"Because you have lived in Japan for a while

and understand our culture well, I thought you knew!" Shiori replied.

But when Shiori and Raymond usually ate together, they always shared the same bowls, cups, and chopsticks.

"Does it bother you that we share?" Raymond asked Shiori.

"Of course not!" Shiori replied. "If it did, I would have told you a long time ago." Then she explained to Raymond that in many Japanese families, it was the custom for each member to have his or her own tableware. In particular, some girls don't want to use the same cups and bowls that their fathers use, Shiori explained. Raymond thought this was sad—and a little strange!

"But doesn't everyone share the same bath water? Isn't that worse than sharing chopsticks?" he thought, but he didn't say anything.

Raymond was happy to learn that having "his bowl" was completely normal in Japanese culture. In fact, he realized that having his own bowl, cup, and chopsticks—just like everyone else—made him part of the family.

2. Getting Along

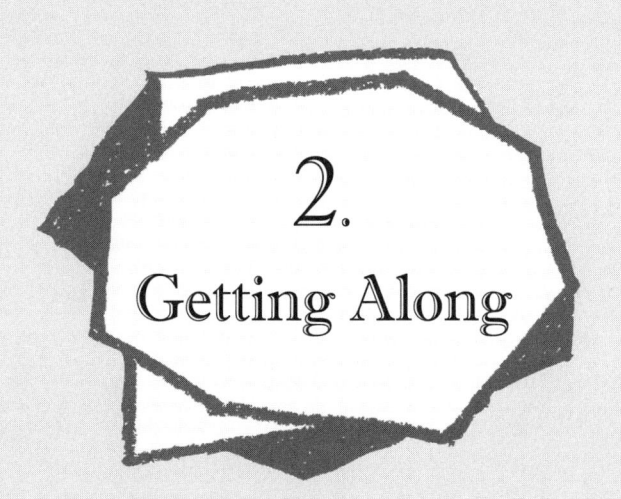

According to Ashley, Japanese people always ask her the same questions. These questions are: "Where are you from? How long have you been in Japan? Why did you come here? And, when are you going back to your country?"

This last question she finds a little rude. "Are people trying to tell me to go home?" she wonders. "It is like asking dinner guests what time they plan to leave as soon as they walk in the door!"

But now that Ashley has heard the question one hundred times, she is used to it. It doesn't bother her so much. "It is just one of the many little things to get used to about living in Japan," she says. And compared to other things, one little question isn't so bad!

Now that Ashley has been in Japan for a few years, there is a new question that people like to ask her. This question is: "Have you gotten used to Japan?"

2. Getting Along

"This question is tricky to answer," explains Ashley. It is impossible for her to answer just "yes" or "no." "This is because the longer you stay in Japan, the harder it gets! The more you understand about the culture, the more rules you start to notice," says Ashley. There are always more and more things to get used to! Just when you've gotten used to one thing, another thing comes along.

Here's an example from Ashley's stay in Japan. Ashley moved to Tokyo from California when she was 22 years old. She had just finished university. At the time, she didn't speak any Japanese. She also didn't really know anything about Japanese culture.

Of course, there are many Japanese people in California. Growing up, Ashley had a few Japanese friends. At their homes, Ashley often ate Japanese food. But together they spoke English. They all played the same American games at school. They watched the same American TV shows. Ashley's friends were pretty "Americanized." So Ashley didn't know just how different people in Japan could be!

When Ashley first came to Japan, she worked

as an English teacher. She lived in a guest house with three other women. Two of the other women were foreign; one was British, and the other was Australian. The third woman, the house manager, was Japanese. Her name was Keiko. Ashley was really happy to be living with a Japanese person. She hoped that Keiko could teach her about Japanese culture. Keiko did teach Ashley—but not quite in the way Ashley had expected or hoped.

Ashley's friends were very important to her. She thought of them as family. She hoped to make friends with her new roommates. A few weeks after she moved in, Ashley decided to have a dinner party. She often had dinner parties in California. Dinner parties, she thought, were a good way to meet old friends and make new friends.

Before planning the party, Ashley asked all her roommates for permission to have a party. Of course, she invited her roommates, too! Everyone said it would be okay. So Ashley invited some teachers from her school.

Ashley spent all day cooking food. Around 7 pm, five of her work colleagues arrived with bottles of wine. Two of her roommates were there, too, but not Keiko. Ashley's work friends and roommates quickly became friends. Soon everyone was enjoying eating and drinking together. Time went by quickly. Nobody noticed that around 9:30 pm, Keiko came home. She had gone silently to her room.

Finally, when the time came for the last train, people begin to leave. Ashley and her roommates stayed up for another hour. They washed the dishes, talked, and finished the wine. Some of the pots were very dirty, so they left them in the sink to soak overnight. Ashley felt very happy as she went to bed—it had been a great party!

The next morning, Ashley slept in. When she finally woke up, she went downstairs to the kitchen. She saw that someone else had cleaned up the pots. This made Ashley feel bad. Someone must have needed to use the pots. She was going to clean them when she got up, but she had slept so late!

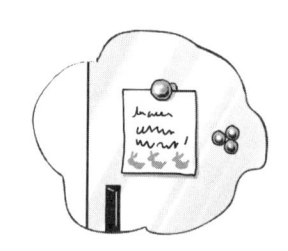

Then, she saw a note on the fridge that said: "Please keep quiet after 10 pm. And clean your own dishes!" The note must be from Keiko, she thought. This made Ashley feel terrible. She didn't want to trouble anyone. That's why she had asked her roommates for permission before having a party! Why didn't Keiko tell her then to be quiet after 10 pm? If Ashley had known, she would have asked her friends to go home at 10 pm.

Ashley quickly went to Keiko's room. She knocked on the door. Keiko opened the door but didn't ask Ashley to come in. In fact, Ashley realized that she had never been inside Keiko's room, even though she had been inside everyone else's room. Ashley stood at the doorway and apologized. Keiko said, "It's okay."

Ashley felt a little bit better. She said to Keiko: "If there is anything else, please tell me!"

2. Getting Along

But Keiko just said: "Don't worry about it."

However, Ashley soon felt very worried. The notes kept coming. Maybe once a week, Ashley would wake up to find a new note.

Here are some examples:

"Please walk up the stairs more quietly."

"Please don't leave your clothes in the washing machine."

"Please wash the pans immediately after using them."

At first, Ashley felt bad. She practiced trying to walk up the stairs without making any noise. They were old wooden stairs, so it was very hard! She learned which stair was the noisiest and tried to skip that one. But Ashley had only forgotten to take her clothes out of the washing machine once. "Was it really necessary to leave a note about that?" she thought. Ashley always washed her dishes after she finished eating. But not before she ate—she didn't want her food to get cold! Surely that made sense? Ashley started to wonder if maybe Keiko should live by herself. She seemed so inflexible!

Ashley wished that Keiko would talk to her in

person. She wished that Keiko would explain the rules to her. Then Ashley wouldn't make any more mistakes! But every time Ashley tried to talk to Keiko, Keiko would say, "It's fine."

Still, Ashley hoped to become friends with Keiko. "I'll try to be extra-helpful," thought Ashley. "Then maybe Keiko will see that I'm not a bad person."

Keiko was the house manager, so it was her job to buy things for the house, like toilet paper. It was also her job to put out the trash and recycling. Because Keiko did these things, she paid less rent than the other women. Ashley decided to help Keiko with the trash and recycling. But she didn't understand the system. It looked very confusing. Ashley asked Keiko to explain it to her. But as usual, Keiko only said, "Don't worry about it." Ashley asked a few times, but still Keiko didn't explain it. So Ashley gave up trying to help. This strategy to win over Keiko wasn't working. Ashley didn't know what else to do.

Some time passed, and Ashley wanted to have another dinner party. She really enjoyed cooking dinner for her friends. "This time, I'll start earlier

2. Getting Along

and have everyone out of the house by 10 pm," she thought. Again, she asked her roommates, and they agreed. Ashley told Keiko that everyone would be gone by 10 pm. She also promised to clean everything before she went to bed. "I hope you'll come this time, Keiko!" said Ashley, smiling.

But Keiko stayed in her room during the party. Ashley tried very hard to keep the party quiet. Many times she reminded her friends to talk more quietly. And at 10 pm, she made everyone go home. Then she cleaned up everything. When it came to vacuuming, though, she wasn't sure what to do because the vacuum would be noisy. So she left a note on the fridge that said: "I'll vacuum in the morning!"

The next morning, Ashley came downstairs and found Keiko in the kitchen. She was cleaning up her breakfast dishes very noisily. It was unusual for Keiko to be noisy. She seemed angry. Ashley asked her if something was wrong. But Keiko just said, "It's okay." Then she left the apartment, slamming the door behind her.

Ashley was so confused! She thought she had done everything right this time.

Over time, however, Ashley learned more about Japanese culture. "I realize now that talking to Keiko directly wasn't a good idea. I should have gotten advice from the Japanese staff at my school."

Now Ashley never has dinner parties. She understands that Japanese houses have thin walls! Instead, she invites her friends to meet at a restaurant or bar. Sometimes, even Keiko comes. "I miss being able to cook for my friends, though. Having a dinner party is different from meeting up in a restaurant. It's so much more comfortable at home!" Ashley says.

2. Getting Along

But Ashley knows better than to bother her roommates or her neighbors. "I'm always concerned that I might be doing something to bother someone else. But I never know for sure because people here won't tell me what they're thinking!

"The longer I live here, the more rules I begin to understand. So there are always more things to worry about! Also, the longer I stay here, the more people expect me to follow the rules. I can't get away with being a newbie anymore! So in a way, even though I'm more used to living in Japan, it is harder," says Ashley. She adds, "I'm happy that I understand Japanese culture better. But on the other hand, I miss the days before I knew the rules! Life was certainly more easygoing then."

3.
Speak Up!

What do English teachers find frustrating about Japanese students? If you ask any English teacher, you'll probably get the same answer: "Japanese students are so afraid to make mistakes!"

Most teachers agree that the best way to learn is to make mistakes. So when students don't make mistakes—or don't talk at all—teachers worry that they aren't learning.

"My students are so shy!" says Chris, an English teacher from Canada. "At first, I thought it was cute. But now I worry that I'm not able to do my job as a teacher."

Chris teaches at a school during the day and gives private lessons in the evening. On his day off, he teaches a class of elderly women at the community center. "Actually, that class is my best class," says Chris. "Those women aren't as shy as the younger students! In fact, they ask me lots of personal questions. It can be a little embarrassing!

3. Speak Up!

"Most of my students are really serious about studying English, which is great," he says. "Very few people in Canada would spend that much time and money studying a second language—even though we have two national languages!"

But some of the students, he says, are a little too serious. They ask him very detailed questions. And some of these questions are hard to answer!

For example: "What is the difference between 'I'd like a hamburger, please' and 'I'll have the hamburger, please?'"

To this question, Chris would answer: "Uh, 'a hamburger' is just a hamburger in general, and 'the hamburger' is specifically the hamburger on the menu."

The dialogue would continue:

Student: "Huh? So which is correct?"

Chris: "They're both correct. You can say either."

Student: "But what do you say?"

Chris: "Uh, I don't know. I probably say both, at different times. But it doesn't matter. Both are okay. Both will get you a hamburger."

At this point, the student would become silent and look confused.

"I feel like I'm letting my students down," says Chris. "But the truth is that both phrases are totally fine. English is a very flexible language. And the goal is just to get the hamburger, right?"

Chris and the other teachers at his school often discuss these topics. Actually, he's discovered that different teachers have different ways of saying things! Sometimes the differences depend on the teacher's native country. Sometimes Chris discovers that men and women have different ways of

3. Speak Up!

saying things. Other times, there is no explanation for the difference! Sometimes native speakers even say things incorrectly just "because that's how they grew up saying it."

"The goal should be communication, not perfection. I don't even think perfect English exists," says Chris.

Certainly, most Westerners' Japanese skills are far from perfect. And most Westerners aren't embarrassed at all about making mistakes in Japanese!

Chris, who is also studying Japanese, explains: "I'm just so happy if I can communicate. Grammar is the last thing on my mind."

However, one thing does bother Chris: "Japanese people never tell me when I make a mistake. I think they don't want to embarrass me. But I wouldn't be embarrassed! I want to improve. And the only way to improve is to learn from your mistakes. As a teacher, I know that!"

He also wonders: "If Japanese people are so worried about perfection, why don't they expect Westerners to speak perfect Japanese? Why do they think it is okay for us to speak imperfect

Japanese, but not okay for them to speak imperfect English? It doesn't make any sense! Why are they harder on themselves than on us?"

Andy, who used to live in Tokyo, but now lives in LA, agrees: "Japanese people are too hard on themselves!"

Recently, Andy's Japanese friend Hiro came to visit him in LA. Hiro had lived in California for a year when he was a student. That was ten years ago. Still, Hiro felt that he should be able to speak English perfectly. Andy and Hiro went to a Mexican restaurant for lunch. Hiro wanted to order by himself, without Andy's help, even though he had trouble understanding the menu. Of course he had trouble—this was a Mexican restaurant, and most of the menu was in Spanish! Hiro tried to read something off the menu. But the waiter couldn't understand him. So in the end, Hiro just pointed to the menu. Afterwards, Andy noticed that Hiro's mood had changed. Hiro was looking down at the table and looked embarrassed.

Andy tried to cheer him up. "It's a Mexican restaurant! The waiters hardly speak English. Don't take it personally," Andy told Hiro. Andy thought

3. Speak Up!

Hiro's reaction was unusual: an American would get mad at the waiter for not understanding. Only a Japanese person would get mad at himself instead, Andy thought.

Chris often hears similar stories from his students who go overseas. "They have to repeat themselves once, and then they feel like a failure. I have to repeat myself all the time in Japanese. It's actually good practice! Too many people treat going overseas like 'show time.' It's not show time. It is still practice. It is always going to be practice."

Chris worries that his students get too nervous, and that affects their ability to communicate. Chris thinks his students need to do more role-playing in class. But his students hate role-play! "It's strange. When I studied French in school, the role-plays were my favorite part," says Chris. "It was fun to play different characters and act silly."

Now that he's a teacher, he says: "If it were up to me, we'd do an hour of role play. That would be the whole lesson. Forget the grammar. But I think all my students would quit!"

Chris also worries that his students are too stiff. He thinks this causes more communication problems than grammar mistakes cause. This is why he thinks so:

"English is a more polite language than you think. It is a different kind of politeness from that of Japanese. There are no special verbs to learn in English. But there is a special attitude, and that is important," explains Chris. "Start every situation with a 'hi' and a smile. This is the way to be polite. And make eye contact, too. In Western culture, making eye contact shows sincerity. You'll be surprised how much smoother things go: at customs, at the rental car counter, at McDonalds. It can be hard at first. But once you get used to it, it becomes natural," he says, adding: "Pretty girls can come up to me and practice anytime they like!"

4. What Are You Calling Me?

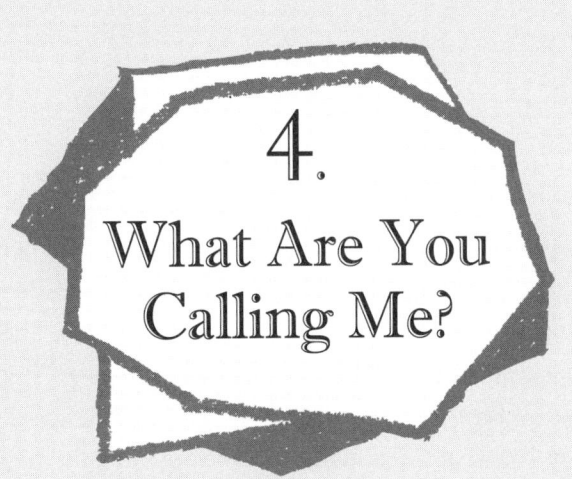

Growing up in America, Leah was called "pinhead." This was because her head was smaller than the other kids in her class. She was called "bug eyes," because of her big, round eyes. She was also called "chicken legs," because of her skinny legs. None of these nicknames was positive. None of them made Leah happy. In fact, they all made Leah feel bad about herself.

Leah was always the shortest, skinniest girl in her class. In her opinion, this wasn't a good thing. The boys in her class didn't think it was a good thing, either. None of the boys in school paid Leah any attention.

The girls that the boys wanted were taller and curvier. They had round faces and big smiles. They had legs shaped by dancing or cheerleading. This wasn't Leah. But that was okay, because Leah was used to it. Leah did well in school instead. She also filled her notebooks with stories and drawings. She often drew funny drawings about her classmates and teachers. She had lots of friends, too. She got along well with other girls—probably because they never got jealous of her.

It wasn't Leah's idea to come to Japan. It was her friend Sharon's idea. Sharon was one of those curvy, popular girls who always had a boyfriend. She had been Leah's best friend since childhood. Sharon had just broken up with her boyfriend, and she wanted a change. Sharon thought it would be fun to spend a year overseas. She asked Leah to come with her. Leah was bored with her job as a research assistant. So the two friends signed up to teach English for a year in Japan. Luckily, they were both assigned to teach in Tokyo, but at different schools.

Leah arrived at her new school. On the first day, she met the Japanese office staff. One of the women looked about Leah's age. When she met Leah, she said, "You have such a small face!"

Leah was hurt. "It's just like school again. They're calling me a pinhead!" she thought. She was also a bit confused. "I thought Japanese people were supposed to be polite. Isn't it rude to make fun of someone's head size?" thought Leah.

But the staff members at her school weren't the only ones to comment on her face size. Her students made the same comment. So did complete strangers. Leah thought it was totally weird.

Also, she didn't know how to respond. Should she say, "Yes, I know," or "I was born that way," or "Thank you"? Was it rude to say, "You do, too" to people who also had a small face? Or was it rude to say, "You have a big face" to someone whose face was bigger than hers? Leah didn't know which was better: to have a small face or a big face.

To tell the truth, Leah had never paid much

4. What Are You Calling Me?

attention to face size. She knew that her own head was kind of small because people teased her and called her "pinhead." But her body was also pretty small, so it seemed like a good match. She didn't think she looked particularly unbalanced.

In America, calling someone a "pinhead" was the same as calling them stupid. Small head equals small brain, get it? But Leah knew that she wasn't stupid. She knew that head size had nothing to do with intelligence. So it must be about appearance, she thought.

So Leah began to study people's faces on the train. She was surprised to learn that there was a big variety of face sizes! After hours of studying faces on the train, Leah never thought, "All Japanese people look the same" again!

One problem remained, however. Leah still couldn't tell which was supposed to be more attractive: the big faces, the medium-sized faces, or the small faces! As far as Leah could tell, there were equally attractive examples of all sizes. She didn't think face size had anything to do with being attractive.

Within a few months of arriving in Japan,

Leah was scouted by a modeling agency. She did some modeling jobs on her day off, to make a little extra money. Leah found modeling and acting to be fun, easy work. She remembered the characters that she used to draw in her notebooks and pretended to be them. When she had to play a princess, for example, she remembered the faces of the mean girls in high school. By the end of the year, Leah was modeling and acting full time.

Can you imagine how surprised Leah was to learn that her small face was attractive to advertisers? And her big bug eyes and skinny chicken legs? Leah was shocked.

"This just proves that beauty is subjective," she says. "Or that Japan is another planet!"

Years later, Leah still studies people's faces on

4. WHAT ARE YOU CALLING ME?

the train. "I want to see if my beauty standard has changed—if I start to see small faces as prettier. But I don't! I still don't get the small face thing," she says. "In fact, if you spend enough time studying faces, you can find something attractive about everyone."

Whatever happened to Leah's friend Sharon? Tall, curvy Sharon had a much different experience. Back in America, Sharon always got attention from men. She was used to getting asked out all the time. But in Japan, not a single guy asked her out! Well, not a single young guy. Shopping in Ginza, she sometimes got mistaken for a bar hostess by older men.

Sometimes, Sharon would try to talk to a Japanese guy at a party. But the guys usually looked at their feet instead of Sharon. Some guys said, "Sorry, I can't speak English." One guy ran away!

Sharon didn't know why the guys in Japan didn't like her. Was she unattractive to them? Was she too tall? Or were they just scared of her? Sharon became lonely. She even started to miss her awful ex-boyfriend in America. Then she became depressed. After her one-year contract at the English school finished, Sharon decided to return to America.

"Poor Sharon! I was so sad when she left," says Leah.

Sharon isn't the only friend that Leah has said good-bye to over the years.

"A lot of my Western female friends only stay a year or two. I am always going to going-away parties! It's sad: now when I make a friend, I expect that she'll be gone soon. Most of them leave for the same reason that Sharon did—they get lonely. You can't expect a girl to go more than a year or two without a boyfriend! And all the Western guys are too busy chasing Japanese girls," Leah says, adding: "Come on, Japanese guys! Talk to us! We're not scary, I promise."

5.
Safety First

If you ask a Western person what they like about Japan, often you will hear the same answer: "It's so safe." That's not to say that Western countries are terribly dangerous. Most likely, you won't get shot or stabbed. But there are small, annoying things that you have to worry about. Like stealing. As most guidebooks will tell you, backpacks are not a good idea; they can easily be opened from behind. Purses should always be zippered—and you wouldn't even buy a purse that didn't have a zipper. And wallet chains aren't just for fashion!

For many Westerners coming to Japan for the first time, it is exciting to walk around with a bag carelessly unzipped. Or a wallet peeking out of a back pocket. It is like having a first sip of alcohol! You know it is bad for you, but you just want to keep going. You want to see how far you can go before you get into trouble.

So many Westerners change their habits when

they come to Japan. Gavin, a Canadian who works for a Japanese advertising firm, is an example. "Over the years, I can feel myself becoming more and more careless," he says. For example, when Gavin first came to Japan, he would never leave his laptop on the table unattended at Starbucks. But now he often does.

"At first, I started leaving it just when I went to the bathroom. But now I put my computer bag on the table—to claim a seat—and leave it there while I go to the counter to order."

"I would never leave my computer like that in Canada," Gavin continues. "Canada isn't as bad as America. But still, you have to be careful. A computer sitting alone like that is just asking to be stolen."

Naturally, Gavin prefers the safety level in Japan. It is very troublesome to bring your computer into the restroom with you!

Once, Gavin left his computer bag in his bicycle basket when he went into the supermarket.

"I didn't even notice that I didn't have my bag. Then I went to pay and realized," Gavin said. "My wallet was in there, too. So I couldn't pay for my groceries.

"I thought for sure that it would be gone. I thought that I had pushed the limit this time."

Gavin dropped his grocery basket and rushed outside. His bag was still there, with both his wallet and computer inside—even though he had left it for twenty minutes!

This really impressed Gavin. He thought that this situation was very different from the situation in Starbucks. At Starbucks, there are always other customers sitting nearby. So a thief might be more afraid of getting caught. But outside the supermarket, people are always coming and going. Nobody would even notice if someone else walked off with Gavin's bag.

"I'm a pretty honest person. But even I might

5. Safety First

be tempted to steal a computer bag left alone like that!" thought Gavin.

Gavin wondered why no one had taken his bag. Was it because Japanese people were really that honest? Was it because everyone in Tokyo who wanted a computer could afford to buy his or her own? Or maybe no one wanted a used computer? Maybe if it had been a new computer in a box, someone would have taken it?

He asked his Western friends what they thought. Many of his friends had similar stories. One American friend, Sarah, told him about the time she left her mobile phone in a family restaurant. Sarah went back the next day and asked the staff if they had found it. The staff took out a box of "lost and found" items. They told her to look through it. Her mobile phone was in the box, as she expected.

But that isn't what surprised her! Sarah realized that she could have taken anything she wanted from the box—including other people's phones. In America, if you lose something, the staff never let you look in the "lost and found" box. Instead, they ask you to describe the item. If there is an item that matches your description, the staff will give it to you. Or else people would lie and steal things all the time!

Sarah also couldn't believe what else was in the restaurant's "lost and found" box. For example, there was an unopened box of cigarettes.

Sarah, who spoke good Japanese, asked the staff: "How long have these been here?"

"I don't know. Awhile. Are they yours?" the staff person replied.

"No... I was just wondering," said Sarah.

"Doesn't anyone who works here smoke?" Sarah thought to herself. "These guys are all part-time workers. Surely nobody here makes a lot of money. Someone should be happy to have a free pack of cigarettes! Besides, nobody is going to come back to the restaurant to claim a pack of cigarettes."

Sarah thought about the "finders keepers" rule in America. This unofficial rule means this: if something small (like a pack of cigarettes) is lost, whoever finds it can keep it. Nobody in America would turn in a pack of cigarettes. And no one in America would go looking for a lost pack of cigarettes.

5. Safety First

Sarah thought about the one thing that she did always lose in Japan: umbrellas. "How come nobody ever returns lost umbrellas?" she asked Gavin. She added, "That would be a lot more useful than a pack of cigarettes."

"Maybe because umbrellas are useful... That's why people take them," thought Gavin. This got Gavin thinking. He decided that he wanted to test just how honest Japanese people really were. He thought of the one thing that was useful to everybody: money.

Since Gavin made pretty good money at the advertising firm, he decided to invest a little bit of his own money in an experiment. On a weekend afternoon, he went to Tokyo Station. In one of the hallways, he "casually" dropped a 10,000 yen note. Then he watched from behind one of the pillars. But nobody picked up the money. Some people stopped briefly to look at it, but then they kept on walking. After a little while, Gavin picked up the money and moved to a different hallway.

"Maybe it wasn't enough money," he thought. This time he "casually" dropped three 10,000 yen notes. He waited and waited. He waited a long time, but still nobody picked up the money.

Finally, a station guard picked up the money and walked over to Gavin.

"I've seen what you've been doing. Please take your money and go home," said the station guard sharply to Gavin.

Gavin was very embarrassed. He put the money in his pocket. With his head low, he headed home.

"I see that Japanese people take their honesty very seriously. I won't question them again!" he thought.

6. Making Friends

Sophia is half Japanese. Her dad is English, and her mom is Japanese. However, Sophia only spoke English growing up. Her whole life she lived in central England, in the countryside. She spent her summer vacations at her grandparents' farm in southern England. In fact, Sophia never even visited Japan until she was 18!

Sophia had grown up thinking she was English. But after that visit to Japan, she started to realize that she had some Japanese qualities too. "I must have learned some things from my mom without realizing it," she thought. Also, she could understand her mom a little bit better. Because of this, she decided that she wanted to understand Japanese culture better.

The next fall, Sophia started university. She decided to study Japanese. She thought she could be a translator like her mom. She wished her mom had taught her more Japanese growing up! Sophia

6. Making Friends

could speak French, because she had studied it in school. She enjoyed studying languages and thought that it would be a new challenge to study Japanese.

For her second year of university, Sophia decided to study in Japan. Her university had an exchange program with a university in Tokyo. Actually, it was a very prestigious women's university!

She was just twenty years old when she arrived in Tokyo. This time she was all by herself, without her mom to help her. Sophia was nervous. But still, she had already spent a year away from home at college. So she was confident that she could manage another year on her own, even in a foreign country.

Sophia was assigned to live in a dormitory with other foreign students. She was surprised by how strict the rules were. For example, there was a 10 pm curfew! Also no boys were allowed in the dormitory. Even though Sophia was still young, she thought, "I'm twenty. I'm an adult. Why am I being treated like a child?"

In the West, only strict religious schools have

curfews. Also, people are considered adults from the age of 18. So Sophia had already had two years to think of herself as an adult. She had been living away from home and was used to making her own rules.

But she had to play by the rules in Japan. This was Sophia's first lesson in the Japanese expression, "There's nothing that can be done." There would, of course, be many more lessons like this. But for foreigners, "There's nothing that can be done" is a very hard lesson! Even though Sophia was half Japanese, she had grown up in England and had a strong feeling of independence.

Sophia quickly made friends with the other foreign students in her dormitory. She had more trouble making friends with the Japanese students.

"Everyone dresses the same. They all carry the same bags. They even say all the same things. I don't know who to talk to. Should I just pick someone at random?" Sophia thought.

Since this was a prestigious women's university, you can imagine that all the young women wore the "correct clothes," carried the "correct bags," and said the "correct things." Of course, this type

6. Making Friends

of young woman also exists in England. But there are also a lot of young women who take pride in looking unique—and Sophia was this type. If Sophia saw someone who dressed like she did, she would go talk to her. But none of the other students wore jeans like Sophia.

Still, Sophia wanted to make friends. She just didn't know how to start. Sophia talked to the advisor for foreign students. She asked for his advice. He suggested that Sophia join one of the university's clubs. Since he knew that Sophia liked music, he suggested that she join the singing club.

Sophia really enjoyed singing. So she thought this was an excellent idea. In fact, Sophia didn't just enjoy singing; she was really good at it. She also played the cello and the piano. She had studied music since she was a little girl. Sophia was really excited that she would be able to practice singing and make friends at the same time. So she quickly joined the singing club.

Sophia was a second-year student and the club's newest member. This meant that she had no seniority in the club. When the members divided up the parts, all the senior girls got the best parts.

Sophia was given the smallest part, even though it was clear that Sophia was a better singer than some of the senior girls.

At first though, Sophia didn't mind. "I'm sure I'll get a better part next time," she thought. "The other girls are just testing me. Once I've proven to them how well I can sing, I'll surely get a better part."

Reading this, you might get the impression that

6. Making Friends

Sophia was arrogant. But that was not the case at all! Sophia was actually pretty modest. There was only one thing that she was confident about: her musical ability. In England, she always got the best parts in the Christmas music show, even when she was a freshman. The custom in the West is to give the best parts to the best people. This is in order to make the best music possible!

Sophia eventually realized that this was not the case in her club. No matter how hard she practiced or how well she sang, Sophia never got a better part. The older girls always took the better parts for themselves. Sophia realized that the only way to get a better part was to belong to the club for many years. But as an exchange student, she would only be in Japan for one year! So she thought the situation was hopeless.

But singing was only one of the reasons that Sophia joined the club. The other goal was to make friends. Fortunately, she was more successful in that. Even though the other girls often teased Sophia for wearing jeans, Sophia felt like she had made friends.

Since she had made some friends, Sophia

decided to quit the singing club. She thought the singing part was a waste of her time. Since she was never given a challenging part, her singing would never improve. Sophia was a hard-working young woman. She didn't want to spend time on something that wasn't challenging. She would rather spend that extra time improving her Japanese! "I'll just go to the social events," Sophia thought. "I can see my friends there."

However, once she quit the club, none of the other members invited her to social events. When Sophia called them, they all said they were too busy. This continued for some time. Finally Sophia realized that when she quit the club, she had also given up her friends! At first, she was confused and hurt. But then she started to think that maybe friendship in Japan had a different meaning from that of friendship in the West.

This made Sophia even more determined to study and understand Japanese culture. In fact, she decided that since she was half-Japanese, she would spend the next half of her life in Japan. This would make herself "even."

Sophia made this decision over ten years ago,

6. Making Friends

and she is still in Japan today! These days, some of her best friends are Japanese. But that doesn't mean she now thinks that making friends is easy. "It takes a lot longer to get to know people in Japan, especially if you meet them later in life," she says. "Japanese people seem to have close friends from their school days. If you miss out on that time together, it can be hard to get close later.

"I guess if I had stayed in that singing club, I would have had friends for life. But I just didn't know how it worked at the time. Instead of trying to prove to them that I was a good singer, I should have been trying to prove to them that I was a good, loyal friend!"

After leaving university, Sophia went on to become a professional singer. In fact, you've probably heard her voice on TV commercials in Japan!

What is the hardest thing for Sophia about living in Japan—even now that she has a good career and good friends? She would say the attitude of "There's nothing that can be done."

"I'm a perfectionist, so it drives me crazy," Sophia says. "But Japanese people are supposed to be perfectionists, too, so I just don't get it!"

7. Opposites Attract

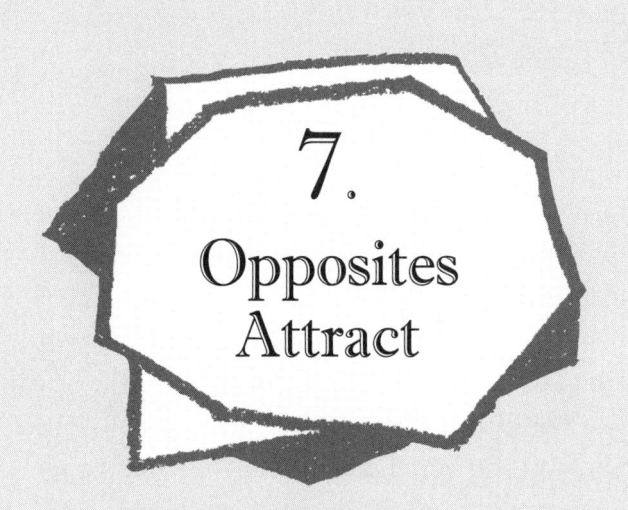

Joanna and Hanako met through language exchange. Joanna was an American English teacher living in Tokyo. She wanted to improve her Japanese ability so that she could talk with Japanese people who didn't speak English. She was bored speaking English all the time at work. She was also bored with having the same simple conversations in English with Japanese people.

Hanako was an office worker who dreamed of one day living overseas. To tell the truth, they didn't have a lot in common; Joanna was really interested in Japanese culture, and Hanako was more interested in American culture than her own.

However, both young women were in their twenties and single. And they did have one thing in common: they both liked going to clubs and dancing. Soon, they started making plans to go for drinks after studying. Soon after that, they stopped studying and started going straight out for drinks.

7. Opposites Attract

Hanako took Joanna to her favorite bars and clubs in Tokyo. Mostly, these were small places in Shibuya and Aoyama where only Japanese people went. Joanna felt special because she was often the only foreign person in the room. She felt like she was experiencing "the real Tokyo."

Joanna was surprised how different the atmosphere was in these nightclubs. Mostly, people seemed to be listening carefully to the DJ. There was some dancing, but not so much. Sometimes guys would look at Joanna and Hanako, and sometimes they would ask Hanako where Joanna was from. But they never talked to Joanna! This made Joanna feel a little bit lonely but also a little bit relieved.

At nightclubs in America, many guys would try to talk to Joanna or dance with her. She felt like she always had to be on guard. If she accidentally made eye contact with a guy, he would soon get the wrong idea and come over. But in these Japanese clubs, she felt very free. She could dance as much as she liked without anyone bothering her! She felt that the Japanese guys who went to nightclubs were very polite.

Jon's Chopsticks

Joanna told Hanako about the difference between Japanese and American nightclubs. After hearing this, Hanako really wanted to experience an American-style club. Of course, it would be too difficult and expensive to fly to America for this reason! So Joanna told Hanako that she would take her out in Roppongi.

Actually, Joanna hated Roppongi. She was embarrassed by the Western guys who hung out there. She thought they were loud and rude. She didn't want to go there at all. However, she felt like she owed it to Hanako to take her since Hanako had taken her to many clubs.

As soon as they got to the club in Roppongi, Hanako headed straight for the dance floor, like

7. Opposites Attract

she always did. And just as Joanna had feared, Hanako was soon surrounded by guys. Hanako let one guy dance closer and closer. Joanna got angry. "Why was Hanako behaving like this?" she wondered. Joanna grabbed her friend and pulled her into the restroom.

"Do you like this guy?" Joanna asked Hanako.

"No!" replied Hanako. "But I don't know what I'm supposed to do."

Joanna laughed. "If you're not interested in him, you have to tell him to go away!"

"Just say, 'go away'? Doesn't that sound rude?" asked Hanako.

At this point, Joanna realized that it wasn't just Western guys who were rude. Western women were rude, too! "But you have to be rude," explained Joanna. "If you're not, the guys won't leave you alone. I told you this would happen!"

Joanna hoped that Hanako would give up on Roppongi. But instead, she became even more determined to master these foreign-style clubs. In fact, Hanako had decided that what she really wanted was a Western boyfriend. Joanna thought she wouldn't mind having a Japanese boyfriend.

So the two decided that they would try to help each other out.

Now these two friends had a shared goal. But it turned out that they had very different taste in men!

Joanna often got annoyed at the Western men she saw in the bars and clubs. Most of them would be talking to beautiful Japanese women. "That guy is not attractive at all," Joanna would complain to Hanako. "Back home, no woman would look twice at him! But in Japan, the women like him just because he's foreign."

Joanna made Hanako promise that she wouldn't go for a guy "just because he was foreign." But actually, Hanako was attracted to exactly the kind of guy Joanna said was unattractive! These guys would be pale and blond, usually skinny, and with "baby faces"—faces that make them look young for their age. According to Joanna, this kind of guy wasn't "masculine" enough. But Hanako thought they were cute!

On the other hand, Hanako couldn't understand why these foreign guys always seemed to be with less attractive Japanese women—women

7. Opposites Attract

whom Joanna thought were beautiful. Joanna was shocked to learn that Hanako didn't think these women were beautiful. It surprised Joanna that people in Japan valued women who looked "more Western"—with round eyes and dyed hair. In America, Asian features were considered beautiful and exotic!

The two friends laughed when they discovered their different definitions of attractiveness.

"It works out perfectly!" thought Joanna. "Western guys who are less attractive to Western women are more attractive to Japanese women. And Japanese women who are less attractive to Japanese men are more attractive to Western men."

Joanna wondered if it worked the other way around with Western women and Japanese men. She just had to figure out how to talk to them!

8.
A Quiet Place

Westerners in Japan seem to be loud. In Japan, their voices can be heard up and down the train. Their hands fly wildly in gestures.

It's not entirely their fault. Growing up in a country with plenty of space creates a totally different way of thinking.

Still, on behalf of all those noisy Westerners with their big suitcases, Ben would like to apologize. "We're not all like that!" he says.

Ben is a big, tall American guy. You probably wouldn't want to sit next to him on the train. Actually, Ben never sits on the train, because he knows he takes up too much space—and also because he still keeps some old Western habits. In the West, men aren't supposed to sit on the train; the seats are for women and old people. Ben gets mad when he sees other Western men sitting on the train; he thinks they've come to Japan and gotten lazy.

8. A Quiet Place

Ben isn't lazy. He works for an IT company. He's always been a shy, quiet, hard-working guy. That's why he loves living in Japan.

"I hope I can stay here forever," he says. "It is so comfortable for me here."

In America, talking is everything. Families sit around the dinner table talking. Friends sit at the bar talking. Parties require mingling and talking to new people. Work requires networking and presenting ideas.

In New York, where Ben went to college, you can hardly cross the street without someone talking to you. Last time Ben went back to visit, a stranger talked to him about rent prices while he waited for the light to change. Ben just smiled and nodded.

Later, he went to a supermarket to buy some cheese. He picked up one kind that looked good to him. A woman shopping nearby told him to pick a different kind instead. Ben didn't know what to do, if he should listen to the woman or ignore her. He just stood there in the cheese aisle holding two pieces of cheese until the woman went away.

Jon's Chopsticks

"Why does everyone in America have to have an opinion about everything?" Ben wondered. He couldn't wait to get back to Japan. There, nobody would talk to him! In fact, they would often try to get out of his way.

In America, talking is considered natural. So if you don't like it—or aren't good at it—people think there is something wrong with you.

At parties in college, people would ask Ben:

"Why so silent? Aren't you having a good time?"

"What's the matter, man? You're so quiet."

"You don't say much, do you?"

These questions stressed Ben out. He was having a good time, just in his own quiet way. He was happy just to listen to what other people were talking about—politics or sports, for example—but he didn't really have an opinion on those things. So he didn't really have anything to say about

8. A Quiet Place

them. And when Ben didn't have anything interesting to say, he preferred not to say it—unlike most Americans!

But still, Ben felt different, and this made him feel sad.

Ben's shy nature also caused problems with dating. In America, the first date always requires lots of conversation. Americans think it is important for couples to have similar opinions and ideas. So during the first few dates, men and women talk about their opinions and ideas to see if they match. Sure, eating good food is important, too, but the conversation is the most important thing. However, Ben would be so stressed about what to say that he couldn't even enjoy the meal!

When he didn't say much, Ben could tell that his date was bored. Or that she was uncomfortable with his silence. "What are you thinking?" she would ask. But Ben could only reply, "Nothing."

Even a movie date was not relaxing for him. This was because he knew that after the movie, he and his date would go to a coffee shop to talk about it. During the movie, he tried to think of interesting things to say.

"This must come naturally to other people," Ben thought. "But not to me."

Ben wished he could meet a woman who was happy just to sit quietly with him. They could enjoy food and movies and the warm space between them—without having to talk about anything.

Ben loved going on dates in Japan. He especially loved dates at Japanese restaurants. He was happy to sit side-by-side at the counter. Sitting face-to-face at a table, there is only the option to talk or stare at the plate of food. It would be weird to just stare silently at each other! But side-by-side at the counter, there is no pressure to talk. Sitting side-by-side, he felt less shy. Ben was happy to discover this way of dining in Japan.

Also, at the counter, Ben and his date could watch the chef work. Ben liked that; he thought it was interesting to see how the food was made. He also liked that the staff explained all the different dishes. Every time a new dish came, it gave him a new conversation topic. Ben liked that!

More than anything, Ben liked that the focus was on eating and not talking.

He loved that Japanese restaurants were so peaceful and quiet. Well, except for the pubs. Ben didn't understand Japanese pub behavior. So quiet one minute, Japanese people suddenly would become so noisy upon entering a pub. In Ben's mind, you were either a quiet person or a noisy person. This was a natural condition, not a social one, he thought.

Ben was naturally a quiet person, so he was pretty much quiet all the time. Whether he was in an expensive restaurant or a cheap pub, Ben stayed the same. He didn't understand this double-personality many Japanese people seemed to have. But he didn't mind. At least they didn't make him feel bad about being quiet and shy.

Something else surprised Ben about Japan. Here, he met other Western people who were just like him—shy and quiet. It seemed like he wasn't the only one who felt more comfortable in Japan!

Ben had always thought that he was unusual. However, in Japan, he learned that there were many quiet and shy people in the world! He felt lucky to have met them. He also felt lucky to have found a place where being quiet and shy is considered natural.

"The world is made up of many different kinds of people. And the world is made up of many different kinds of places," Ben says. "It is great when the people and the places match. But sometimes they don't. When that happens, people should travel to find the place that suits them. That's what I did, and I'm so much happier.

"I know there must be some Japanese people who don't match Japan. Maybe they like to talk a lot and have strong opinions. These people should try America!" says Ben.

9.
City Life

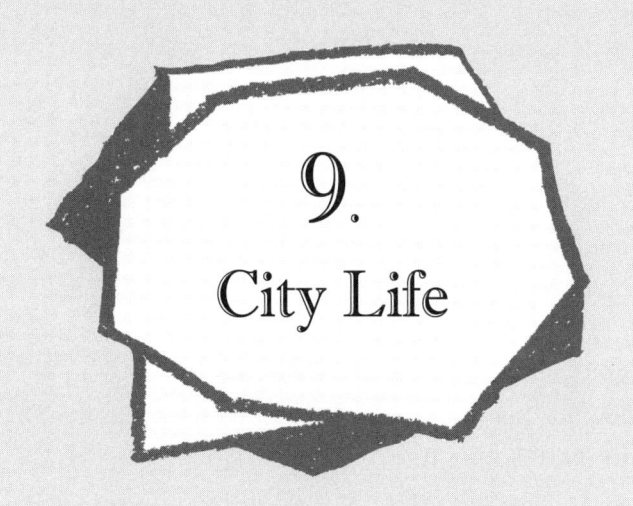

When people ask Casey how she feels about living in Japan, she has one answer: "I live in Tokyo, not Japan. I can't tell you anything about Japan."

Casey has lived in Tokyo for five years. She grew up on the east coast of America, in a small town. After graduating from university, she lived in New York City for a few years. She worked as an assistant editor at a publishing house. She worked long hours. Each year, she had only two weeks of holiday. One week she spent visiting her family. The other week she spent traveling. Casey wished she could travel more. Casey wished that she could travel and work at the same time.

Casey decided to leave New York and move to Tokyo. Living in a foreign country, she thought, would be similar to traveling and working at the same time. Casey started out working as an English teacher at an English conversation school. She hated it.

9. CITY LIFE

"I felt like the school was more interested in making money than teaching students," she said. "The students learned very little English. The teachers made very little money. And the school made lots of money. I couldn't wait to get out of there."

After a few months, Casey found another job editing translations. With her background in publishing, this was a good match for her. "Working as an English teacher, I felt like a clown, like I was performing for students, trying to entertain them. But now that I have a normal desk job, I feel like a normal person again."

Casey loved her new life in Tokyo. She had her own apartment. The rent, she says, is similar to that in New York. "My room is a little bit smaller. But everything is so modern, I love it. I love the bath—it's digital. It talks!" she says.

She finds Japanese people easy to get along with. "They're honest, polite, and most importantly, quiet. Americans talk too much! And it is always about themselves. Whenever I go to a bar, I can always tell if there are Americans on the other side of the room," she says.

Jon's Chopsticks

Just don't ask Casey if she is an English teacher. "It drives me crazy! Why do all Japanese people assume anyone who speaks English is an English teacher? We can do other things, too, you know? Not just speaking our own native language. Some of us actually have careers."

"Can you imagine if I asked a Japanese businessman in New York if he was a Japanese teacher?" says Casey, laughing.

When Casey has a holiday, she likes to travel to other Asian countries. She's been to Thailand, Bali, India, and Vietnam.

"I love that these places are so close," she says. "It would be too far to fly to Asia from New York. When I lived in New York, I often traveled to Europe. But Europe is so stiff and old. Asian cities are younger, more exciting. And I love the tropical weather! Plus, traveling in Asia is much cheaper than traveling in Europe."

Casey spends most of her money on traveling. She hardly spends money on clothes. "I'm more interested in experience than things," says Casey.

Recently, Casey has started to travel around the countryside in Japan. She realized that even

9. CITY LIFE

though she lived in Japan, she didn't really "know" Japan. After all, she spent all her time in Tokyo!

"In America, the difference between the cities and the countryside is huge! It is almost like two different countries." Casey knows this well; she had lived in both a small country town and New York City.

Casey realized that it was easy for her to adjust to life in Tokyo after adjusting to life in New York. "The two cities really aren't that different," she says. "In both, you can walk anywhere or take the subway. Supermarkets, restaurants, and bars stay open late, even all night. The people who live in the next apartment to you might be strangers. But you make friends with the people who hang out at the local bar."

Also, Tokyo has a diverse population. Not as diverse as New York, of course, but diverse for Japan. Says Casey: "In Tokyo, I can have Japanese friends and American friends. I can also have friends from other Asian countries and friends from Europe."

After traveling around the Japanese countryside, Casey wonders if Tokyo has more in common with New York than the rest of Japan. "I could see similarities between Tokyo and New York, and similarities between the Japanese countryside and the American countryside. But Tokyo and the Japanese countryside seemed like night and day—completely different.

In Tokyo, Casey often goes out to restaurants and bars by herself. Casey often sees other single women in restaurants and bars. The waiters and bartenders always treat her with kindness. Nobody makes her feel bad about being alone. "I feel like it is totally okay to be a single woman in Tokyo," she says. "It is probably better to be a single woman in Tokyo than in New York actually, since it is much safer in Tokyo."

However, when Casey traveled outside the city, she had a completely different experience. Last September, Casey decided to visit some of the Izu Islands (okay, these are still Tokyo, but very different!) She visited each of the inner islands. Each night, she stayed on a different island. She slept in small inns run by local families. On one island, the woman at the inn was very chatty. She asked Casey many questions, including, "How old are

9. City Life

you? Do you have a boyfriend? Do you want to get married? What do your parents think of your living so far away?"

Casey told the woman that she was single. She also said that she didn't know if she wanted to get married. The woman looked sad for Casey. She said to Casey, "Aren't you lonely?"

This question made Casey uncomfortable. Of course, she got lonely sometimes. But on the other hand, there was no fighting. There was no one to tell her what to do. Casey had had boyfriends who made her feel lonelier than being alone. But she didn't want to explain this to the woman.

"Uh, sometimes," she said, and hurried to her room.

Casey left the hotel the next morning. She thanked the woman for the comfortable room and the good food. The woman smiled and replied: "I hope you come again. Next time, I hope you come with your husband."

Casey knew then that she would never go back to that inn! She knew the woman was trying to be nice. But Casey felt so uncomfortable! She felt like she was back in her small hometown in

America again—the same town that she left when she moved to New York.

Casey has another story from her travels around Japan. One time, her parents came to visit her in Japan. They decided to travel to Nagano and Gifu. They rented a car. At first, Casey drove. But she was out of practice from living in cities so long. So Casey's dad took over driving. Casey sat in the passenger seat and helped her dad with directions. This was a good arrangement. Casey was the only one in the car who could read the signs! Casey's mom sat in the back seat.

At one point, they stopped to get gas. The gas station attendant began talking to Casey's dad. Casey's dad shrugged his shoulders and pointed to Casey. Casey asked the gas attendant for "a full tank of regular." When the attendant was finished pumping the gas, he told Casey's dad how much to pay. Again, Casey did the talking and gave the man some money. When he returned with the change, he brought it to Casey's dad and said thank you.

"The whole time I was talking, the gas station attendant never looked at me. It was like I didn't exist! He kept looking at my dad and talking to my dad. I guess that was because he was the man? Or maybe it was because he was older? It was so strange!"

The same thing happened when Casey's family checked into hotels. The hotel staff would speak Japanese to Casey's dad. Even when it was clear that only Casey could speak Japanese, the staff continued to talk to her dad. "My family thought it was really funny. Of course, my dad wouldn't care if the staff spoke to me instead of him. My dad is always the responsible one, so it would be a nice break for him actually!

"I like traveling in the countryside," says Casey. "It is really beautiful. But I'm always happy to come back to my life in Tokyo!"

10. Closing Doors

People around the world are impressed with Japanese people's politeness. When foreign tourists return home, they tell their friends and family: "Japanese people are so kind and polite." If you ask for directions, someone won't just tell you; they'll walk you to your destination. If they cannot help you with directions, they will apologize seriously, maybe with a bow.

Also, Japanese people are always giving compliments. For example:

"You speak Japanese so well!"

"You look like David Beckham!"

Westerners really and truly do believe that Japanese people are polite. Most believe that Japanese people are more polite than people in their own country! You won't get compliments on your language ability in a Western country. Somebody might give you directions. Or they might say "sorridunno" (that's "I'm sorry I don't know" said very

10. Closing Doors

fast!) and turn away."

Most foreign people are happy to live in such a polite country—a country more polite than they could ever have imagined possible. Japan even encourages them to try harder to be more polite. What a good thing!

"If only every place in the world could be this polite," foreign visitors to Japan think.

Then a door hits them in the face.

This happens to every single Western person at least once. It is a great shock. Getting hit in the face by a door is not such a shock. It is a surprise, but one that is quickly over. But getting hit in the face by a door in "the most polite country in the world" is a shock. It is a very big shock that causes Western people deep confusion.

In Western countries, it is the custom to hold the door open for someone coming behind you. "It's a habit. You do it without even thinking about it," explains Dave, an American in Tokyo. "I don't really think of myself as a polite person. But I always hold the door open. It's just natural."

Dave explains this natural process: "When you pass through the door, look quickly behind you to see if anyone is following. If there is someone following, keep your hand on the door until the other person reaches it. Then the following person puts out his or her hand to catch the door. This continues from person to person."

"It's kind of like a relay race," says Dave. "The door gets handed to each person coming."

The only exception is a woman with a baby stroller. If the person behind you is a woman (or

10. Closing Doors

man!) with a baby stroller, it is the custom to hold the door open wide and let that person pass through. This is so that the person pushing the stroller doesn't have to bother with the door.

"I guess we do this because we feel sympathy for the woman. It must be very hard to hold the door and push a baby stroller at the same time! And what if the door hit the stroller? That would be terrible," says Dave.

Dave wonders: "Why don't Japanese people hold the door open for each other? They do so many other things that are more polite than this! Why not do this one simple little thing? Like I said, I don't think I am a very polite person. But at least I do this. It's easy!"

"I guess politeness means different things in different cultures," continues Dave. "For example, in Japan, it is okay to pick your nose in public, but not blow your nose. In America it is the opposite; you can blow your nose in public, but you can't pick. But when you think about it, they're both equally gross."

Or maybe it isn't a question of politeness at all, Dave wonders. "Maybe people in Tokyo are too used to automatic doors? Or because traditional sliding doors don't hit people in the face like Western doors? So they never developed a habit of holding open the door for people? I don't know!"

Dave had been in Japan for about a week when the first door slammed in his face. He had expected the person in front of him to hold the door, but that person didn't. Dave was right behind the person. So he literally walked right into the door!

"I felt really stupid," says Dave. "I must have looked like an idiot. But still, I thought this must have been an exception. It took a few more doors for me to learn my lesson."

Still, it is hard for Dave to break his habit. He still holds the door open for people.

"Really, I'm not trying to be nice. It's just a habit. But some people seem really surprised by it. Then they bow and say thank you! I feel guilty, like I don't really deserve their thanks!"

Sometimes, however, this habit causes confusion. As Dave explains: the point isn't to hold the door all the way—just to hold the door until the next person can put their hand out to catch it.

10. Closing Doors

But since people in Japan don't have this custom, sometimes they don't reach for the door!

"I've found myself holding the door open for several people in a row. They just keep coming. I don't want the door to hit anyone. So I just keep standing there holding the door. Once, I must have held the door open for about twenty women. They must have thought it was my job!"

Dave wonders if he should give up holding the door, or if he should continue.

"I'd like to take the best from both cultures. Take the things that are good about American culture and the things that are good about Japanese culture and put them together: that would be best. I think it is nice to hold the door open for people; it's friendly. But on the other hand, doing so makes me stand out. It makes me feel more like a foreigner."

"Anyway," Dave says, "I'm happy there are so many automatic doors in Japan, so I don't have to worry about it too much."

Word List

- 本文で使われている全ての語を掲載しています（LEVEL 1、2）。ただし、LEVEL 3 以上は、中学校レベルの語を含みません。
- 語形が規則変化する語の見出しは原形で示しています。不規則変化語は本文中で使われている形になっています。
- 一般的な意味を紹介していますので、一部の語で本文で実際に使われている品詞や意味と合っていないことがあります。
- 品詞は以下のように示しています。

名 名詞	代 代名詞	形 形容詞	副 副詞	動 動詞	助動 助動詞
前 前置詞	接 接続詞	間 間投詞	冠 冠詞	略 略語	俗 俗語
頭 接頭語	尾 接尾語	記 記号	関 関係代名詞		

A

- ☐ **a year or two** 1～2年
- ☐ **ability** 名 ①できること、(～する)能力 ②才能
- ☐ **accidentally** 副 偶然に、誤って
- ☐ **according** 副《- to ～》～によれば［よると］
- ☐ **act** 動 ①行動する ②機能する ③演じる
- ☐ **actually** 副 実際に、本当に、実は
- ☐ **add** 動 ①加える、足す ②言い添える
- ☐ **adjust** 動 ①適応する［させる］、慣れる ②調整する
- ☐ **adult** 名 大人、成人
- ☐ **advertiser** 名 広告主
- ☐ **advertising** 名 広告、宣伝
- ☐ **advice** 名 忠告、助言、意見
- ☐ **advisor** 名 忠告者、助言者、顧問
- ☐ **affect** 動 影響する
- ☐ **afford** 動《can -》～することができる、～する(経済的・時間的な)余裕がある
- ☐ **after all** やはり、結局
- ☐ **after that** その後
- ☐ **afterwards** 副 その後、のちに
- ☐ **agency** 名 代理店
- ☐ **aisle** 名 通路、側廊
- ☐ **alcohol** 名 アルコール
- ☐ **all** 熟 after all やはり、結局 all by oneself 自分だけで、独力で all the time ずっと、いつも、その間ずっと all the way ずっと not ～ at all 少しも[全然]～ない
- ☐ **allow** 動 ①許す、《- … to ～》…が～するのを可能にする、…に～させておく ②与える
- ☐ **alone** 熟 leave ～ alone ～をそっとしておく
- ☐ **along** 熟 get along やっていく、はかどる get along with (人)と仲良くする、気[うま]が合う、歩調を合わせる
- ☐ **America** 名 アメリカ《国名・大陸》
- ☐ **American** 形 アメリカ(人)の 名 アメリカ人
- ☐ **American-style** 形 アメリカ式の
- ☐ **Americanized** 形 アメリカ化されている
- ☐ **Andy** 名 アンディ《人名》
- ☐ **angry** 熟 get angry 腹を立てる

Word List

- **annoyed** 形 困って, イライラして
- **annoying** 形 人を悩ます, いらいらさせる
- **any more** 《not ~》もう［これ以上］~ない
- **anymore** 副《通例否定文, 疑問文で》今はもう, これ以上, これから
- **anyone** 代 ①《疑問文・条件節で》誰か ②《否定文で》誰も (~ない) ③《肯定文で》誰でも
- **anything else** ほかの何か
- **anytime** 副 いつでも
- **anyway** 副 ①いずれにせよ, ともかく ②どんな方法でも
- **anywhere** 副 どこかへ［に］, どこにも, どこへも, どこにでも
- **apartment** 名 アパート
- **apologize** 動 謝る, わびる
- **appearance** 名 ①現れること, 出現 ②外見, 印象
- **appreciate** 動 ~の良さが分かる, ~をありがたく思う
- **arrangement** 名 ①準備, 手配 ②取り決め, 協定 ③整頓, 配置
- **arrogant** 形 尊大な, 傲慢な, 無礼な, 横柄な
- **as** 熟 as far as one can できるだけ as much as ~と同じだけ as usual いつものように, 相変わらず just as (ちょうど)であろうとおり see ~ as … ~を…と考える
- **Ashley** 名 アシュレイ《人名》
- **Asia** 名 アジア
- **Asian** 名 アジア人 形 アジアの
- **ask ~ if** ~かどうか尋ねる
- **asleep** 形 眠って (いる状態の) fast asleep ぐっすり眠っている
- **assign** 動 任命する, 割り当てる
- **assistant** 名 助手, 補佐 形 援助の, 補佐の
- **assume** 動 ①仮定する, 当然のことと思う ②引き受ける
- **atmosphere** 名 ①大気, 空気 ②雰囲気
- **attendant** 名 つき添い人, 案内係, アテンダント
- **attention** 名 ①注意, 集中 ②配慮, 手当て, 世話
- **attitude** 名 姿勢, 態度, 心構え
- **attract** 動 ①引きつける, 引く ②魅力がある, 魅了する
- **attractive** 形 魅力的な, あいきょうのある
- **attractiveness** 名 人を引き付ける［魅了する］こと
- **Australia** 名 オーストラリア《国名》
- **Australian** 形 オーストラリアの 名 オーストラリア人
- **automatic** 形 自動の, オートマチックの
- **away** 熟 go away 立ち去る not get away with ただではすまない run away 走り去る, 逃げ出す turn away 向こうへ行く, 追い払う, (顔を)そむける, 横を向く
- **awful** 形 ①ひどい, 不愉快な ②恐ろしい
- **awhile** 副 しばらくの間

B

- **back** 熟 come back to ~へ帰ってくる, ~に戻る get back 戻る, 帰る go back to ~に帰る［戻る］, ~に遡る, (中断していた作業に)再び取り掛かる put back (もとの場所に)戻す, 返す
- **background** 名 背景, 前歴, 生い立ち
- **backpack** 名 バックパック, リュックサック
- **Bali** 名 バリ《インドネシア》
- **bar** 名 酒場, バー

JON'S CHOPSTICKS

- **bartender** 名 バーテンダー
- **bathroom** 名 ①浴室 ②手洗い, トイレ
- **beauty** 名 ①美, 美しい人[物] ②《the -》美点
- **because of** 〜のために, 〜の理由で
- **behalf** 利益 on behalf of 〜のために, 〜に代わって
- **behave** 動 振る舞う
- **behavior** 名 振る舞い, 態度, 行動
- **behind** 前 ①〜の後ろに, 〜の背後に ②〜に遅れて, 〜に劣って 副 ①後ろに, 背後に ②遅れて, 劣って
- **belong** 動《-to 〜》〜に属する, 〜のものである
- **Ben** 名 ベン《人名》
- **besides** 副 その上, さらに
- **better** 熟 know better (than)(〜より)もっと分別がある
- **bit** 名 ①小片, 少量 ②《a-》少し, ちょっと
- **blond** 形 金髪の, ブロンドの, (皮膚が)色白の
- **blow** 動 ①(風が)吹く, (風が)〜を吹き飛ばす ②息を吹く, (鼻を)かむ blow one's nose 鼻をかむ
- **bored** 動 bore (退屈させる)の過去, 過去分詞 形 うんざりした, 退屈した
- **bother** 動 悩ます, 困惑させる
- **bow** 動 (〜に)お辞儀する
- **bowl** 名 どんぶり, わん
- **boyfriend** 名 男友だち
- **brain** 名 ①脳 ②知力
- **break up with** (恋人などの関係が)壊れる, 別れる
- **briefly** 副 短く, 簡潔に
- **British** 形 ①英国人の ②イギリス英語の 名 英国人
- **bug** 名 小虫 bug eyes 出目
- **businessman** 名 ビジネスマン, 実業家

C

- **California** 名 カリフォルニア《米国の州》
- **can** 熟 as far as one can できるだけ can hardly とても〜できない can't help 避けられない, 〜せずにはいられない There's nothing that can be done. 仕方がない。
- **Canada** 名 カナダ《国名》
- **Canadian** 形 カナダ(人)の 名 カナダ人
- **cannot** can (〜できる)の否定形(=can not)
- **career** 名 ①(生涯の・専門的な)職業 ②経歴, キャリア
- **careless** 形 不注意な, うかつな
- **carelessly** 副 不注意にも, ぞんざいに
- **Casey** 名 ケーシー《人名》
- **casually** 副 何気なく, 軽い気持ちで, 偶然に
- **caught** 熟 get caught 逮捕される
- **cello** 名 チェロ
- **central** 形 中央の, 主要な
- **certainly** 副 確かに, 必ず
- **challenge** 名 ①挑戦 ②難関
- **challenging** 形 能力が試される, やる気をそそる
- **character** 名 ①特性, 個性 ②(小説・劇などの)登場人物 ③文字, 記号 ④品性, 人格
- **chase** 動 ①追跡する, 追い[探し]求める ②追い立てる
- **chatty** 形 話し好きな
- **check** 動 ①照合する, 検査する ②(所持品を)預ける check into (ホテルに)チェックインする
- **cheer up** 元気になる, 気分が引き

WORD LIST

立つ
- **cheerleading** 名チアリーディング, チアリーダーの活動
- **cheese** 名チーズ
- **chef** 名シェフ, 料理長
- **childhood** 名幼年[子ども]時代
- **chopsticks** 名はし
- **Chris** 名クリス《人名》
- **Christmas** 名クリスマス
- **cigarette** 名(紙巻)たばこ
- **claim** 動①主張する ②要求する, 請求する
- **clear** 形はっきりした, 明白な
- **close** 熟 closer and closer どんどん近づく get close 近づく
- **clown** 名道化(役者), おどけ者
- **coast** 名海岸, 沿岸
- **colleague** 名同僚, 仲間, 同業者
- **come** 熟 come along ①一緒に来る, ついて来る ②やって来る, 現れる ③うまくいく, よくなる, できあがる come back to ～へ帰ってくる, ～に戻る come on ①いいかげんにしろ, もうよせ, さあ来なさい ②(人)に偶然出会う come over やって来る, ～の身にふりかかる come up 近づいてくる, 階上に行く, 浮上する, 水面へ上ってくる, 発生する, 芽を出す how come どうして, なぜ
- **comfortable** 形快適な, 心地いい
- **comment** 名論評, 解説, コメント 動論評する, 注解する, コメントする
- **commercial** 名コマーシャル
- **common** 熟 in common (with) (～と)共通して
- **communicate** 動①知らせる, 連絡する ②理解し合う
- **communication** 名伝えること, 伝導, 連絡
- **community** 名団体, 共同社会, 地域社会 community center コミュニティ・センター, 公民館
- **compare** 動比較する, 対照する
- **complain** 動不平[苦情]を言う, ぶつぶつ言う
- **complete** 形完全な, まったくの
- **completely** 副完全に, すっかり
- **complicated** 形①複雑な ②むずかしい, 困難な
- **compliment** 名①賛辞, 敬意 ②《-s》あいさつ
- **concern** 動心配する, (人)にとって気になる
- **condition** 名①(健康)状態, 境遇 ②《-s》状況, 様子 ③条件
- **confident** 形自信のある, 自信に満ちた
- **confused** 形困惑した, 混乱した
- **confusing** 形混乱させる, 紛らわしい
- **confusion** 名混乱(状態)
- **consider** 動①考慮する, ～しようと思う ②(～と)みなす ③気にかける, 思いやる
- **contaminate** 動汚染する, 汚す
- **contract** 名契約(書)
- **conversation** 名会話, 会談
- **correct** 形正しい, 適切な, りっぱな
- **could have done** ～だったかもしれない《仮定法》
- **counter** 名(店の)売り台, カウンター
- **countryside** 名地方, 田舎
- **couple** 名夫婦, 一組
- **crazy** 形①狂気の, ばかげた, 無茶な ②夢中の, 熱狂的な
- **create** 動創造する, 生み出す, 引き起こす
- **cupboard** 名食器棚, 戸棚
- **curfew** 名門限

- curvy 形 曲線美の
- customer 名 顧客

D

- dancing 名 ダンス, 舞踏
- Dave 名 デーヴ《人名》
- David Beckham デビッド・ベッカム《イギリス出身のサッカー選手, 1975–》
- day 熟 one day（過去の）ある日,（未来の）いつか these days このごろ
- deal 名 取引, 扱い
- decade 名 10年間
- decision 名 ①決定, 決心 ②判決
- definition 名 定義, 限定
- depend 動《 – on [upon] ~》①~を頼る, ~をあてにする ②~による
- depress 動 憂鬱にする
- depressed 形 がっかりした, 落胆した
- describe 動（言葉で）描写する, 特色を述べる, 説明する
- description 名（言葉で）記述（すること）, 描写（すること）
- deserve 動（~を）受けるに足る, 値する,（~して）当然である
- destination 名 行き先, 目的地
- detailed 形 詳細な, 詳しい
- determined 形 決心した, 決然とした
- develop 動 ①発達する［させる］ ②開発する
- dialogue 名 対話, 話し合い
- digital 形 数字の, 数字表示の, デジタルの
- dining 名 食事, 夕食をとること
- direction 名 ①方向, 方角 ②《-s》指示, 説明書 ③指導, 指揮
- directly 副 ①じかに ②まっすぐに ③ちょうど
- dirty 形 汚い, 汚れた
- discuss 動 議論［検討］する
- diverse 形 ①種々の, 多様な ②異なった
- divide 動 分かれる, 分ける, 割れる, 割る
- DJ 略 ディスク・ジョッキー《= disc jockey》
- do well 成績が良い, 成功する
- done There's nothing that can be done. 仕方がない。
- doorway 名 戸口, 玄関, 出入り口
- dormitory 名 寄宿舎, 寮
- double 形 ①2倍の, 二重の ②対の
- double-personality 名 二重人格
- downstairs 名 階下
- draw 動 ①引く, 引っ張る ②描く ③引き分けになる［する］
- drawing 名 ①素描, 製図 ②引くこと
- drew 動 draw（引く）の過去
- driving 名 運転
- drove 動 drive（車で行く）の過去
- dyed 形 染めた

E

- each other お互いに
- easily 副 ①容易に, たやすく, 苦もなく ②気楽に
- easygoing 形 あくせくしない, のんびりした
- edit 動 編集する
- editor 名 編集者, 編集長
- either A or B A かそれとも B
- elderly 形 かなり年配の, 初老の

WORD LIST

- **else** 熟 anything else ほかの何か or else さもないと
- **embarrass** 動 恥ずかしい思いをさせる, 困らせる
- **embarrassed** 形 恥ずかしい, 当惑して
- **embarrassing** 形 恥ずかしい, きまりが悪い, 当惑させる
- **encourage** 動 ①勇気づける ②促進する, 助長する
- **end** 熟 in the end とうとう, 結局, ついに
- **England** 名 ①イングランド ②英国
- **entertain** 動 ①もてなす, 接待する ②楽しませる
- **entirely** 副 完全に, まったく
- **equal** 動 匹敵する, 等しい
- **equally** 副 等しく, 平等に
- **Europe** 名 ヨーロッパ
- **even** 形 等しい, 公平な, おあいこの
- **even though** 〜であるけれども, 〜にもかかわらず
- **eventually** 副 結局は
- **every time** 〜するときはいつも
- **everybody** 代 誰でも, 皆
- **everyone** 代 誰でも, 皆
- **everything** 代 すべてのこと[もの], 何でも, 何もかも
- **ex-boyfriend** 名 以前つき合っていた彼氏
- **excellent** 形 優れた, 優秀な
- **except** 前 〜を除いて, 〜のほかは except for 〜を除いて, 〜がなければ
- **exception** 名 例外, 除外, 異論
- **excited** 形 興奮した, わくわくした
- **exciting** 形 興奮させる, わくわくさせる
- **exist** 動 存在する, 生存する, ある, いる
- **exotic** 形 異国風の, 魅惑的な, 外来の
- **expect** 動 予期[予測]する, (当然のこととして)期待する
- **experiment** 名 実験, 試み
- **explanation** 名 ①説明, 解説, 釈明 ②解釈, 意味
- **expression** 名 ①表現, 表示, 表情 ②言い回し, 語句
- **extra** 形 余分の, 臨時の
- **extra-** 頭 〜外の, 並外れた

F

- **face-to-face** 副 面と向かって, 直接に
- **fact** 熟 in fact つまり, 実は, 要するに
- **failure** 名 ①失敗, 落第 ②不足, 欠乏 ③停止, 減退
- **far** 熟 as far as one can できるだけ far away 遠く離れて far from 〜から遠い, 〜どころか how far どのくらいの距離ですか so far 今までのところ, これまでは
- **fashion** 名 ①流行, 方法, はやり ②流行のもの(特に服装)
- **fast asleep** ぐっすり眠っている
- **fault** 名 ①欠点, 短所 ②過失, 誤り
- **fear** 動 ①恐れる ②心配する
- **feature** 名 ①特徴, 特色 ②顔の一部, 《-s》顔立ち
- **feel like** 〜がほしい, 〜したい気がする, 〜のような感じがする not feel like doing 〜する気になれない
- **feeling** 名 ①感じ, 気持ち ②触感, 知覚 ③同情, 思いやり, 感受性
- **female** 形 女性の, 婦人の, 雌の
- **fighting** 名 戦闘

- **figure** 動 ①描写する, 想像する ②計算する ③目立つ, (～として) 現れる **figure out** 理解する, ～であるとわかる, (原因などを) 解明する
- **finders keepers** 拾ったものは自分のもの
- **firework** 名 花火
- **firm** 名 会社, 事務所
- **first** 熟 **at first** 最初は, 初めのうちは **for the first time** 初めて
- **flexible** 形 ①(物が)曲がりやすい, しなやかな ②(考えなどが)柔軟性のある, 順応性のある ③(予定・計画などが)融通のきく ④弾力的な, 可塑性のある
- **fluent** 形 流ちょうな, 流れる(ような)
- **focus** 名 ①焦点, ピント ②関心の的, 着眼点 ③中心
- **following** 形 《the –》次の, 次に続く
- **foreign-style** 形 洋風の
- **foreigner** 名 外国人, 外国製品
- **fork** 名 フォーク
- **fortunately** 副 幸運にも
- **free-spirited** 形 自由奔放な性格の
- **freedom** 名 ①自由 ②束縛がないこと
- **freeze** 動 凍り付く, こわばる
- **French** 形 フランス(人・語)の 名 ①フランス語 ②《the –》フランス人
- **freshman** 名 1年生, 新人
- **fridge** 名 冷蔵庫
- **friend** 熟 **make friends with** ～と友達になる
- **friendly** 形 親しみのある, 親切な, 友情のこもった
- **friendship** 名 友人であること, 友情
- **front** 熟 **in front of** ～の前に, ～の正面に
- **frustrating** 形 苛立たしい, もどかしい, 失望させる
- **fun** 熟 **make fun of** ～を物笑いの種にする, からかう
- **funny** 形 ①おもしろい, こっけいな ②奇妙な, うさんくさい

G

- **gas** 名 ガソリン
- **Gavin** 名 ギャビン《人名》
- **general** 熟 **in general** 一般に, たいてい
- **get** 熟 **get a job** 職を得る **get along with** (人)と仲良くする, 気[うま]が合う, 歩調を合わせる **get along** やっていく, はかどる **get angry** 腹を立てる **get asked out** デートに誘われる **get away with** うまく逃れる, やり過ごす **get back** 戻る, 帰る **get caught** 逮捕される **get close** 近づく **get into trouble** 面倒を起こす, 困った事になる, トラブルに巻き込まれる **get it** 理解する, 納得する **get mad at** ～に腹を立てる **get out of** ～から下車する, ～から取り出す, ～から外へ出る[抜け出る] **get to** (事)を始める, ～に達する[到着する] **get to know** 知るようになる, 知り合う **get up** 起き上がる, 立ち上がる **get used to** ～になじむ, ～に慣れる **not get away with** ただではすまない
- **girlfriend** 名 女友だち
- **give up** あきらめる, やめる, 引き渡す **give up on** ～に見切りをつける
- **go** 熟 **go away** 立ち去る **go back to** ～に帰る[戻る], ～に遡る, (中断していた作業に)再び取り掛かる **go by** ①(時が)過ぎる, 経過する ②～のそばを通る ③～に基づいて[よって]行う **go doing** ～をしに行く **go for** ～に出かける, ～を追い求める, ～を

WORD LIST

好む **go on to** ～に移る, ～に取り掛かる **go on** 続く, 続ける, 進み続ける, 起こる, 発生する **go out** 外出する, 外へ出る

- [ ] **going-away party** 歓送会, 送別会
- [ ] **good** 熟 be good at ～が得意だ have a good time 楽しい時を過ごす
- [ ] **good-bye** 間 さようなら 名 別れのあいさつ
- [ ] **gotten** 動 get (得る) の過去分詞
- [ ] **grab** 動 ①ふいにつかむ, ひったくる ②横取りする
- [ ] **graduate** 動 卒業する
- [ ] **grammar** 名 文法
- [ ] **grandparent** 名 祖父母
- [ ] **grateful** 形 感謝する, ありがたく思う
- [ ] **grocery** 名 ①食料雑貨店 (=grocery store) ②《-ies》食料品
- [ ] **gross** 形 ひどい, (食べ物が)粗末な, 不快な
- [ ] **grow up** 成長する, 大人になる
- [ ] **guard** 名 ①警戒, 見張り ②番人
- [ ] **guest** 名 客, ゲスト
- [ ] **guest house** 多国籍賃貸住居
- [ ] **guidebook** 名 旅行[観光]案内書, ガイドブック, 手引き
- [ ] **guilty** 形 有罪の, やましい
- [ ] **guy** 名 男, やつ 《you -s で呼びかけにも用いる》

H

- [ ] **habit** 名 習慣, 癖, 気質
- [ ] **half-Japanese** 名 日系のハーフ
- [ ] **hallway** 名 玄関, 廊下
- [ ] **hamburger** 名 ハンバーガー
- [ ] **hand** 熟 hand out 配る on the other hand 一方, 他方では
- [ ] **hang out** よく行く, 入りびたる
- [ ] **happen to** たまたま～する, 偶然～する
- [ ] **happy to do** 《be -》～してうれしい, 喜んで～する
- [ ] **hard to** ～し難い
- [ ] **hard-working** 形 よく働く, 勤勉な
- [ ] **hardly** 副 ①ほとんど～でない, わずかに ②厳しく, かろうじて can hardly とても～できない
- [ ] **hate** 動 嫌う, 憎む, (～するのを)いやがる
- [ ] **have** 熟 have a good time 楽しい時を過ごす have nothing to do with ～と何の関係もない could have done ～だったかもしれない《仮定法》 should have done ～すべきだった(のにしなかった)《仮定法》
- [ ] **having** 動 have (持つ) の現在分詞, 動名詞
- [ ] **hear from** ～から手紙[電話・返事]をもらう
- [ ] **help** 熟 can't help 避けられない, ～せずにはいられない help each other out 互いに助け合う help ～ with … …を～の面で手伝う
- [ ] **here are ～** こちらは～です。
- [ ] **hi** 間 おい, やあ
- [ ] **home** 熟 at home 自宅で, 在宅して
- [ ] **hometown** 名 生まれ故郷, 出身地
- [ ] **honest** 形 ①正直な, 誠実な, 心からの ②公正な, 感心な
- [ ] **honesty** 名 正直, 誠実
- [ ] **hopeless** 形 ①希望のない, 絶望的な ②勝ち目のない
- [ ] **hostess** 名 女主人, 女性司会者
- [ ] **how** 熟 how come どうして, なぜ how far どのくらいの距離ですか no matter how どんなに～であろう

とも
- **however** 副 たとえ〜でも 接 けれども, だが
- **huge** 形 巨大な, ばく大な
- **huh** 間《驚き・困惑・軽蔑・疑問などを表して》ふん, なんだって
- **hung** 動 hang (かかる) の過去, 過去分詞

I

- **idiot** 名 ばか, まぬけ
- **if** 熟 ask 〜 if 〜かどうか尋ねる if only 〜でありさえすれば see if 〜かどうかを確かめる what if もし〜だったらどうなるだろうか wonder if 〜ではないかと思う
- **ignore** 動 無視する, 怠る
- **imagine** 動 想像する, 心に思い描く
- **immediately** 副 すぐに, 〜するやいなや
- **imperfect** 形 不完全な, 未完成な
- **importantly** 副 重大に, もったいぶって
- **impress** 動 印象づける, 感銘させる
- **impression** 名 ①印象, 感想 ②感動
- **improve** 動 改善する[させる], 進歩する
- **including** 前 〜を含めて, 込みで
- **incorrectly** 副 間違って, 不正確に
- **independence** 名 独立心, 自立
- **India** 名 インド《国名》
- **Indonesia** 名 インドネシア《国名》
- **inflexible** 形 柔軟性のない, 融通のきかない
- **inn** 名 宿屋, 居酒屋
- **inner** 形 ①内部の ②心の中の
- **instead** 副 その代わりに instead of 〜の代わりに, 〜をしないで
- **intelligence** 名 ①知能 ②情報
- **interested** 形 興味を持った, 関心のある be interested in 〜に興味[関心]がある
- **interesting** 形 おもしろい, 興味を起こさせる
- **invest** 動 投資する, (金・精力などを)注ぐ
- **It is 〜 for someone to ...** (人)が…するのは〜だ
- **It takes someone 〜 to ...** (人)が…するのに〜(時間など)がかかる
- **item** 名 ①項目, 品目 ②(新聞などの)記事

J

- **Japan** 名 日本《国名》
- **Japanese** 形 日本(人・語)の 名 ①日本人 ②日本語
- **jealous** 形 嫉妬して, 嫉妬深い, うらやんで
- **jeans** 名 ジーンズ, ジーパン
- **Joanna** 名 ジョアンナ《人名》
- **job** 熟 get a job 職を得る
- **Jon** 名 ジョン《人名》
- **just as** (ちょうど)であろうとおり

K

- **keep on 〜[-ing]** 〜し続ける, 繰り返し〜する
- **keeper** 名 保護者, 後見人
- **kind of** ある程度, いくらか, 〜のような物[人]
- **kindness** 名 親切(な行為), 優しさ

Word List

- **knives** 名 knife (ナイフ) の複数
- **knock** 動 ノックする, たたく, ぶつける
- **know** 熟 get to know 知るようになる, 知り合う know better (than) (〜より) もっと分別がある

L

- **LA** 略 ロサンゼルス《= Los Angeles》
- **language exchange** ランゲージ・エクスチェンジ《お互いに自分の国の言葉を相手に教えること》
- **laptop** 名 ラップトップコンピュータ, ノート型パソコン
- **lazy** 形 怠惰な, 無精な
- **Leah** 名 リア《人名》
- **learn one's lesson** 教訓を得る, 失敗から学ぶ
- **least** 名 最小, 最少 at least 少なくとも
- **leave ~ alone** 〜をそっとしておく
- **leave ~ for ...** …を〜のために残しておく
- **less** 形 〜より小さい [少ない] 副 〜より少なく, 〜ほどでなく
- **lesson** 熟 learn one's lesson 教訓を得る, 失敗から学ぶ
- **let down** 期待を裏切る, 失望させる
- **level** 名 水準
- **lie** 動 うそをつく
- **like** 熟 feel like 〜がほしい, 〜したい気がする, 〜のような感じがする would like to 〜したいと思う
- **likely** 副 たぶん, おそらく
- **limit** 名 限界, 《-s》範囲, 境界
- **literally** 副 文字どおり, そっくりそのまま
- **live on** 〜を糧として生きる
- **living** 名 生計, 生活 make a living 生計を立てる, 自活する
- **lonely** 形 ①孤独な, 心さびしい ②ひっそりした, 人里離れた
- **look down at** 〜に目 [視線] を落とす
- **look for** 〜を探す
- **look through** 〜をのぞき込む
- **look to** 〜しようとする
- **lost and found** 遺失物取扱い
- **loyal** 形 忠実な, 誠実な
- **luckily** 副 運よく, 幸いにも

M

- **mad** 熟 get mad at 〜に腹を立てる
- **made up** 《be –》〜で構成されている
- **make** 熟 make ~ stand out 〜を目立たせる make a living 生計を立てる, 自活する make friends with 〜と友達になる make fun of 〜を物笑いの種にする, からかう make money お金を儲ける make noise 音を立てる make sense 意味をなす, よくわかる make up 作り出す, 考え出す, 〜を構成 [形成] する
- **make-up** 名 化粧 (品), メーク, メーキャップ
- **maker** 名 作る人, メーカー rice maker 炊飯器
- **Malaysia** 名 マレーシア《国名》
- **manage** 動 ①動かす, うまく処理する ②経営 [管理] する, 支配する ③どうにか〜する
- **manager** 名 経営者, 支配人, 支店長, 部長
- **married** 動 marry (結婚する) の過去, 過去分詞 形 結婚した, 既婚の
- **masculine** 形 男らしい, 力強い

JON'S CHOPSTICKS

- **master** 動修得する
- **match** 名相手, 釣り合うもの 動調和する, 釣り合う
- **matter** 熟 not matter 問題にならない no matter how どんなに〜であろうとも
- **McDonalds** 名マクドナルド《ファストフードチェーン店》
- **mean** 形意地悪な
- **meaning** 名①意味, 趣旨 ②重要性
- **medium-sized** 形 Mサイズの, 中型の
- **meet up** 会う
- **menu** 名メニュー, 献立表
- **Mexican** 形メキシコ(人)の 名メキシコ人
- **might** 助《mayの過去》①〜かもしれない ②〜してもよい, 〜できる
- **mind** 名①心, 精神, 考え ②知性 動①気にする, いやがる ②気をつける, 用心する
- **mingle** 動入り混じる, 混ざる
- **miso soup** みそ汁
- **miss out** (チャンス・楽しい事などを)逃す
- **mobile phone** 携帯電話
- **model** 動(ファッションの)モデルをする
- **modeling** 名(ファッション)モデル業
- **modern** 形現代[近代]の, 現代的な, 最近の
- **modest** 形控えめな, 謙虚な
- **money** 熟 make money お金を儲ける
- **mood** 名気分, 機嫌, 雰囲気, 憂うつ
- **more** 熟 not 〜 any more もう[これ以上]〜ない
- **mostly** 副主として, 多くは, ほとんど
- **mother-in-law** 名姑, 義母
- **move in** 引っ越す
- **move to** 〜に引っ越す
- **much** 熟 as much as 〜と同じだけ
- **musical** 形音楽の

N

- **national** 形国家[国民]の, 全国の
- **native** 形①出生(地)の, 自国の ②(〜に)固有の, 生まれつきの, 天然の
- **naturally** 副生まれつき, 自然に, 当然
- **nearby** 副近くで, 間近で
- **necessary** 形必要な, 必然の
- **nervous** 形①神経の ②神経質な, おどおどした
- **network** 名回路, 網状組織, ネットワーク
- **New York** ニューヨーク《米国の都市; 州》
- **New Zealand** ニュージーランド《国名》
- **newbie** 名初心者, 新入り
- **next to** 〜のとなりに, 〜の次に
- **nickname** 名愛称, あだ名
- **nightclub** 名ナイトクラブ
- **no one** 誰も[一人も]〜ない
- **nobody** 代誰も[1人も]〜ない
- **nod** 動うなずく, うなずいて〜を示す
- **noise** 名騒音, 騒ぎ, 物音 make noise 音を立てる
- **noisily** 副音を立てて, 騒々しく
- **noisy** 形①騒々しい, やかましい ②けばけばしい
- **none** 代(〜の)何も[誰も・少しも]…ない

Word List

- **normal** 形 普通の, 平均の, 標準的な
- **nose** 熟 blow one's nose 鼻をかむ pick one's nose 鼻をほじる
- **not** 熟 not ~ any more もう[これ以上]~ない not ~ at all 少しも[全然]~ない not feel like doing ~する気になれない not get away with ただではすまない not matter 問題にならない not quite まったく~だというわけではない
- **note** 名 ①メモ, 覚え書き ②紙幣
- **notebook** 名 ノート, 手帳
- **nothing** 熟 have nothing to do with ~と何の関係もない nothing but ただ~だけ, ~にすぎない, ~のほかは何も…ない There's nothing that can be done. 仕方がない。
- **notice** 動 ①気づく, 認める ②通告する
- **now that** 今や~だから, ~からには

O

- **off** 形 休みの
- **okay** 形 《許可, 同意, 満足などを表して》よろしい, 正しい
- **once a week** 週に一回
- **one day** (過去の)ある日, (未来の)いつか
- **one-year** 形 1年間の
- **oneself** 熟 all by oneself 自分だけで, 独力で by oneself 一人で, 自分だけで, 独力で for oneself 独力で, 自分のために
- **only** 熟 if only ~でありさえすれば
- **opposite** 名 反対の人[物]
- **option** 名 選択(の余地), 選択可能物, 選択権
- **order** 熟 in order to ~するために, ~しようと
- **other hand** on the other hand 一方, 他方では
- **out** get asked out デートに誘われる get out of ~から下車する, ~から取り出す, ~から外へ出る[抜け出る] out of ①~から外へ, ~から抜け出して ②~から作り出して, ~を材料として ③~の範囲外に, ~から離れて ④(ある数)の中から out of practice 腕がなまって, 下手な take out 取り出す, 取り外す, 連れ出す, 持って帰る take out of ~から出す, ~に連れ出す turn out ~と判明する
- **over time** 時間とともに, そのうち
- **overnight** 副 一晩中, 夜通し
- **overseas** 形 海外の, 外国の 副 海外へ 名 国外
- **owe** 動 ①(~を)負う, (~を人の)お陰とする ②(金を)借りている, (人に対して~の)義務がある
- **own** 熟 of one's own 自分自身の on one's own 自力で

P

- **pack** 名 包み, 荷物
- **pale** 形 ①(顔色・人が)青ざめた, 青白い ②(色が)薄い, (光が)薄暗い
- **pan** 名 平なべ, フライパン
- **parent** 名 ①《-s》両親 ②先祖
- **part-time** 形 パートタイムの, 非常勤の
- **particular** 名 事項, 細部, 《-s》詳細 in particular 特に, とりわけ
- **particularly** 副 特に, とりわけ
- **pass through** ~を通る, 通行する
- **passenger** 名 乗客, 旅客
- **pay** 動 ①支払う, 払う, 報いる, 償う ②割に合う, ペイする

JON'S CHOPSTICKS

- **peaceful** 形 平和な, 穏やかな
- **peek** 動 ちらっと見る, のぞき見する
- **perfection** 名 完全, 完成
- **perfectionist** 名 完全[完璧]主義者
- **perfectly** 副 完全に, 申し分なく
- **perform** 動 ①(任務などを)行う, 果たす, 実行する ②演じる, 演奏する
- **permission** 名 許可, 免許
- **person** 熟 in person (本人)自ら, 自身で
- **personal** 形 ①個人の, 私的な ②本人自らの
- **personality** 名 人格, 個性
- **personally** 副 個人的には, 自分で
- **phrase** 名 句, 慣用句
- **pick one's nose** 鼻をほじる
- **pick up** 拾い上げる
- **pillar** 名 ①柱, 支柱, 支え ②根幹
- **pinhead** 名 ①頭が異常に小さい人 ②ばか, 愚か者
- **plate** 名 (浅い)皿, 1皿の料理
- **play by the rules** ルールに従って行動する
- **plenty** 名 十分, たくさん, 豊富 plenty of たくさんの〜
- **plus** 副 その上
- **pm** 略 午後(= post meridiem)
- **point** 熟 at this point 現時点で
- **polite** 形 ていねいな, 礼儀正しい, 洗練された
- **politeness** 名 丁寧さ, 慇懃
- **politics** 名 政治(学), 政策
- **population** 名 人口, 住民(数)
- **positive** 形 肯定的な, 好意的な
- **possible** 形 ①可能な ②ありうる, 起こりうる
- **pot** 名 (深い)なべ

- **practice** 熟 out of practice 腕がなまって, 下手で
- **prefer** 動 (〜のほうを)好む, (〜のほうが)よいと思う
- **presentation** 名 ①提出, 提示 ②実演, プレゼンテーション
- **pressure** 名 プレッシャー, 圧力, 圧縮, 重荷
- **prestigious** 形 世評の高い, 名声のある
- **pretend** 動 ①ふりをする, 装う ②あえて〜しようとする
- **price** 名 ①値段, 代価 ②《-s》物価, 相場
- **pride** 名 誇り, 自慢, 自尊心
- **princess** 名 王女
- **private** 形 私的な, 個人の
- **probably** 副 たぶん, あるいは
- **process** 名 ①過程, 経過, 進行 ②手順, 方法, 製法, 加工
- **professional** 形 専門の, プロの, 職業的な
- **prove** 動 ①証明する ②(〜であることが)わかる, (〜と)なる
- **proven** 動 prove (証明する)の過去分詞
- **pub** 名 酒場, パブ
- **public** 名 一般の人々, 大衆 in public 人前で, 公然と
- **publishing** 名 出版(業)
- **purse** 名 ①財布, 小銭入れ ②小物入れ
- **put** 熟 put back (もとの場所に)戻す, 返す put down 下に置く, 下ろす put in 〜の中に入れる put on ①〜を身につける, 着る ②〜を…の上に置く put out ①外に出す, (手など)を(差し)出す ②(明かり・火を)消す

Word List

Q

- **quality** 名 ①質, 性質, 品質 ②特性 ③良質
- **quickly** 副 敏速に, 急いで
- **quietly** 副 ①静かに ②平穏に, 控えめに
- **quit** 動 やめる, 辞職する, 中止する
- **quite** 熟 not quite まったく〜だというわけではない

R

- **random** 形 手当たり次第の, 無作為の　at random 手当たり次第, 無作為に
- **rather** 副 ①むしろ, かえって ②かなり, いくぶん, やや ③それどころか逆に　would rather 〜する方がよい
- **Raymond** 名 レイモンド《人名》
- **reach for** 〜に手を伸ばす, 〜を取ろうとする
- **reaction** 名 反応, 反動, 反抗, 影響
- **read off** 読み取る
- **realize** 動 理解する, 実現する
- **recently** 副 近ごろ, 最近
- **recycling** 名 リサイクリング
- **regular** 形 ①規則的な, 秩序のある ②定期的な, 一定の, 習慣的
- **relax** 動 ①くつろがせる ②ゆるめる, 緩和する
- **relay** 名 交替, リレー, 中継
- **relieved** 形 安心した, ほっとした
- **religious** 形 ①宗教の ②信心深い
- **remain** 動 ①残っている, 残る ②(〜の)ままである [いる]
- **remind** 動 思い出させる, 気づかせる
- **rent** 動 賃借りする 名 使用料, 賃貸料
- **rental** 形 賃貸の, レンタルの
- **repeat** 動 繰り返す
- **reply** 動 答える, 返事をする, 応答する
- **require** 動 ①必要とする, 要する ②命じる, 請求する
- **research** 名 調査, 研究
- **respond** 動 答える, 返答[応答]する
- **responsible** 形 責任のある, 信頼できる, 確実な
- **restroom** 名 (デパート, レストランなどの)化粧室, トイレ
- **return to** 〜に戻る, 〜に帰る
- **rice maker** 炊飯器
- **role** 名 ①(劇などの)役 ②役割, 任務
- **role-play** 名 役割練習
- **role-playing** 名 ロール・プレーイング, 役割演技
- **roommate** 名 ルームメイト, 部屋を共有する相手
- **row** 名 (横に並んだ)列　in a row 1列に(並んで), 連続して
- **rude** 形 粗野な, 無作法な, 失礼な
- **rule** 熟 play by the rules ルールに従って行動する
- **run away** 走り去る, 逃げ出す
- **rush** 動 突進する, せき立てる

S

- **safety** 名 安全, 無事, 確実
- **salary** 名 給料
- **Sarah** 名 サラ《人名》
- **scared** 動 scare (こわがらせる)の過去, 過去分詞　be scared of 〜を恐れる
- **scary** 形 恐ろしい, こわい, 臆病な
- **scout** 動 スカウトする

JON'S CHOPSTICKS

- **second-year student** 2年生
- **see ~ as …** ~を…と考える
- **see if** ~かどうかを確かめる
- **seem** 動(~に)見える, (~のように)思われる **seem to be** ~であるように思われる
- **senior** 形年長の, 年上の, 古参の, 上級の
- **seniority** 名年功序列, 年長
- **sense** 名①感覚, 感じ ②《-s》意識, 正気, 本性 ③常識, 分別, センス ④意味 **make sense** 意味をなす, よくわかる
- **serious** 形①まじめな, 真剣な ②重大な, 深刻な, (病気などが)重い
- **seriously** 副①真剣に, まじめに ②重大に
- **settle** 動①安定する[させる], 落ち着く, 落ち着かせる ②《- in ~》~に移り住む, 定住する **settle down** 落ち着く, 興奮がおさまる
- **shape** 動形づくる, 具体化する
- **shared goal** 共通の目標
- **Sharon** 名シャロン《人名》
- **sharply** 副鋭く, 激しく, はっきりと
- **shocked** 形ショックを受けて, 憤慨して, 驚いて
- **short** 形 **in short** 要約すると
- **should have done** ~すべきだった(のにしなかった)《仮定法》
- **shoulder** 名肩
- **shrug** 動(肩を)すくめる
- **shy** 形内気な, 恥ずかしがりの, 臆病な
- **shyly** 副はにかんで, 内気に
- **side** 名側, 横, そば, 斜面
- **side-by-side** 形隣り合って
- **silence** 名沈黙, 無言, 静寂
- **silent** 形①無言の, 黙っている ②静かな, 音を立てない

- **silently** 副静かに, 黙って
- **silly** 形おろかな, 思慮のない
- **similar** 形同じような, 類似した, 相似の **similar to**《be -》~に似ている
- **similarity** 名類似(点), 相似
- **sincerity** 名正直, 誠実
- **singer** 名歌手, シンガー
- **singing** 名歌うこと, 歌声
- **single** 形①たった1つの ②独身の
- **sink** 名(台所の)流し
- **sip** 名(酒などの)ひと口, ちびちび飲むこと
- **situation** 名①場所, 位置 ②状況, 境遇, 立場
- **skill** 名①技能, 技術 ②上手, 熟練
- **skinny** 形骨と皮ばかりの, やせた
- **skip** 動(途中を)抜かす, 飛ばす
- **slam** 動ばたんと閉まる, 急に閉める
- **sleep in** 寝床に入る, 朝寝坊する, 住み込む
- **sliding door** 引き戸
- **slightly** 副わずかに, いささか
- **slowly** 副遅く, ゆっくり
- **smoke** 動喫煙する, 煙を出す
- **smooth** 形滑らかな, すべすべした
- **sneak** 動①こそこそする ②こっそり持ち出す, くすねる **sneak out of** ~からこっそり抜け出す
- **so ~ that** 非常に~なので…
- **so far** 今までのところ, これまでは
- **so that** ~するために, それで, ~できるように
- **soak** 動浸す
- **social** 形①社会の, 社会的な ②社交的な, 愛想のよい
- **some time** いつか, そのうち
- **somebody** 代誰か, ある人

Word List

- **someone** 代 ある人, 誰か
- **something** 代 ①ある物, 何か ②いくぶん, 多少
- **sometimes** 副 時々, 時たま
- **Sophia** 名 ソフィア《人名》
- **southern** 形 南の, 南向きの, 南からの
- **Spanish** 形 スペイン(人・語)の 名 ①スペイン人 ②スペイン語
- **speak up** 率直に話す, はっきりしゃべる
- **speaker** 名 ①話す人, 演説者, 代弁者 ②スピーカー, 拡声器 ③議長
- **specifically** 副 特に, 明確に, 具体的に
- **stab** 動 (突き)刺す
- **staff** 名 職員, スタッフ
- **stair** 名 (階段の)1段
- **stand out** 突き出る, 目立つ
- **standard** 名 標準, 規格, 規準
- **Starbucks** 名 スターバックス《コーヒーショップ名》
- **stare** 動 じっと[じろじろ]見る
- **stay in** 家にいる, (場所)に泊まる, 滞在する
- **stay up** 起きている, 夜更かしする
- **stay with** ～の所に泊まる
- **steal** 動 盗む
- **stealing** 名 窃盗
- **stiff** 形 ①堅い, 頑固な ②堅苦しい
- **stolen** 動 steal (盗む)の過去分詞
- **stranger** 名 ①見知らぬ人, 他人 ②不案内[不慣れ]な人
- **strategy** 名 戦略, 作戦, 方針
- **stress out** ストレスを感じさせる, イライラさせる
- **stressed** 動 ストレスを受ける
- **stressful** 形 ストレスの多い
- **strict** 形 厳しい, 厳密な
- **stroller** 名 折りたたみ式の乳母車
- **stupid** 形 ばかな, おもしろくない
- **subjective** 形 主観(的)な
- **subway** 名 地下鉄, 地下道
- **successful** 形 成功した, うまくいった
- **such a** そのような
- **suggest** 動 ①提案する ②示唆する
- **suit** 動 ①適合する[させる] ②似合う
- **suitcase** 名 スーツケース
- **supermarket** 名 スーパーマーケット
- **support** 名 ①支え, 支持 ②援助
- **suppose** 動 ①仮定する, 推測する ②《be -d to ~》～することになっている, ～するものである
- **sure** 熟 for sure 確かに
- **surely** 副 確かに, きっと
- **surprised** 形 驚いた be surprised to do ～して驚く
- **surround** 動 囲む, 包囲する
- **sympathy** 名 ①同情, 思いやり, お悔やみ ②共鳴, 同感

T

- **tableware** 名 食器類
- **take** 熟 take a trip 旅行する take off (衣服を)脱ぐ, 取り去る, ～を取り除く, 離陸する, 出発する take out 取り出す, 取り外す, 連れ出す, 持って帰る take out of ～から出す, ～に連れ出す take over 引き継ぐ, 支配する, 乗っ取る take up 取り上げる, 拾い上げる, やり始める, (時間・場所を)とる
- **tank** 名 タンク
- **taste** 名 ①味, 風味 ②好み, 趣味
- **tease** 動 いじめる, からかう, 悩ま

JON'S CHOPSTICKS

- □ tell ~ to ... ~に…するように言う
- □ tell the truth 《to-》実は、実を言えば
- □ tempt 動 誘う、誘惑する、導く、心を引きつける
- □ terribly 副 ひどく
- □ Thailand 名 タイ《国名》
- □ thank ~ for ~に対して礼を言う
- □ that 熟 after that その後 so ~ that … 非常に~なので… so that ~するために、それで、~できるように
- □ There's nothing that can be done. 仕方がない。
- □ these days このごろ
- □ thief 名 泥棒、強盗
- □ thin 形 薄い、細い
- □ think of ~のことを考える、~を思いつく、考え出す
- □ thinking 名 考えること、思考
- □ though 接 ①~にもかかわらず、~だが ②たとえ~でも 副 しかし
- □ throw up 跳ね上げる
- □ time 熟 all the time ずっと、いつも、その間ずっと at the time そのころ、当時は every time ~するときはいつも for some time しばらくの間 for the first time 初めて have a good time 楽しい時を過ごす over time 時間とともに、そのうち some time いつか、そのうち
- □ toilet 名 トイレ、化粧室
- □ Tokyo 名 東京《地名》
- □ topic 名 話題、見出し
- □ totally 副 全体的に、すっかり
- □ tourist 名 旅行者、観光客
- □ trading company 貿易会社、商社
- □ traditional 形 伝統的な
- □ translation 名 翻訳、言い換え、解釈
- □ translator 名 翻訳者、通訳者
- □ trash 名 ①くず、ごみ ②くだらないもの[人]
- □ treat 動 扱う
- □ tricky 形 油断のならない、扱いにくい、ずるい
- □ trip 熟 take a trip 旅行する
- □ tropical 形 熱帯の
- □ trouble 熟 get into trouble 面倒を起こす、困った事になる、トラブルに巻き込まれる
- □ troublesome 形 面倒な、やっかいな
- □ truly 副 ①全く、本当に、真に ②心から、誠実に
- □ trust 動 信用[信頼]する、委託する
- □ truth 名 ①真理、事実、本当 ②誠実、忠実さ to tell the truth 実は、実を言えば
- □ turn away 向こうへ行く、追い払う、(顔を)そむける、横を向く
- □ turn in 届け出る
- □ turn out ~と判明する
- □ twenties 名 20歳代

U

- □ uh 間 えー、ええと
- □ unattended 形 無人の
- □ unattractive 形 魅力のない、美しくない
- □ unbalanced 形 ①不均衡な、アンバランスな、不安定な ②取り乱した、錯乱した
- □ uncomfortable 形 心地よくない
- □ unique 形 唯一の、ユニークな、独自の

Word List

- **university** 名(総合)大学
- **unlike** 前 ～と違って
- **unofficial** 形 非公式の
- **unopened** 形 未開封の
- **unthinkable** 形 考えられない
- **unusual** 形 普通でない, 珍しい, 見[聞き]慣れない
- **unzipped** 形 ジッパー[ファスナー]の閉まっていない
- **up to** ①～まで, ～に至るまで, ～に匹敵して ②《be-》～の責任[義務]である
- **upon** 前 ①《場所・接触》～(の上)に ②《日・時》～に ③《関係・従事》～に関して, ～について, ～して 副 前へ, 続けて
- **used** 動《-to》よく～したものだ, 以前は～であった 形 ①慣れている, 《get [become] -to》～に慣れてくる ②使われた, 中古の
- **usual** 形 通常の, いつもの, 平常の, 普通の as usual いつものように, 相変わらず

V

- **vacuum** 名 ①真空, 空白 ②電気掃除機 動 電気掃除機で掃除する
- **value** 動 高く評価する, 尊ぶ
- **variety** 名 ①変化, 多様性, 寄せ集め ②種類
- **verb** 名 動詞
- **Vietnam** 名 ベトナム《国名》
- **visitor** 名 訪問客

W

- **wait a long time** 長時間待つ
- **wait for** ～を待つ
- **waiter** 名 ウェイター, 給仕
- **wake up** 起きる, 目を覚ます wake up to ～に気付く, ～で目を覚ます
- **walk around** 歩き回る, ぶらぶら歩く
- **walk off** 立ち去る
- **walk up** 歩み寄る, 歩いて上る
- **walk over to** ～の方に歩いていく
- **wallet** 名 札入れ
- **washing machine** 洗濯機
- **way** 熟 all the way ずっと in a way ある意味では way of ～する方法 way to ～する方法
- **week** 熟 once a week 週に一回
- **weird** 形 変わった, 妙な, 奇妙な
- **well** 熟 do well 成績が良い, 成功する
- **well-paying** 形 給料のよい
- **western** 形 ①西の, 西側の ②《W-》西洋の
- **westerner** 名 西洋人, 欧米人
- **what if** もし～だったらどうなるだろうか
- **whatever** 代 ①《関係代名詞》～するものは何でも ②どんなこと[もの]が～とも 形 ①どんな～でも ②《否定文・疑問文で》少しの～も, 何らかの
- **whenever** 接 ①～するときはいつでも, ～するたびに ②いつ～しても
- **whether** 接 ～かどうか, ～かまたは…, ～であろうとなかろうと
- **while** 熟 for a while しばらくの間, 少しの間
- **whoever** 代 ～する人は誰でも, 誰が～しようとも
- **whole** 形 全体の, すべての, 完全な, 満～, 丸～ 名《the-》全体, 全部
- **whom** 代 ①誰を[に] ②《関係代名詞》～するところの人, そしてその

人を
- □ **wide** 形幅の広い, 広範囲の, 幅が～ある 副広く, 大きく開いて
- □ **wildly** 副荒々しく, 乱暴に, むやみに
- □ **win over** 説得する, 口説き落とす
- □ **wine** 名ワイン, ぶどう酒
- □ **within** 前①～の中[内]に, ～の内部に ②～以内で, ～を越えないで 副中[内]へ[に], 内部に 名内部
- □ **woke** 動 wake (目が覚める) の過去
- □ **wonder** 動①不思議に思う, (～に) 驚く ②(～かしらと) 思う wonder if ～ではないかと思う
- □ **wooden** 形木製の, 木でできた
- □ **work** 熟 at work 働いて, 仕事中で work out うまくいく, 何とかなる, (問題を) 解く, 考え出す, 答えが出る, ～の結果になる work on ～で働く, ～に取り組む
- □ **worker** 名仕事をする人, 労働者
- □ **working** 形働く, 作業の, 実用的な
- □ **worried** 形心配そうな, 不安げな
- □ **worse** 形いっそう悪い, より劣った, よりひどい
- □ **would like to** ～したいと思う
- □ **would rather** ～する方がよい
- □ **wrong with** 《be－》(～にとって) よくない, ～が故障している

Y・Z

- □ **year or two** 《a－》1～2年
- □ **zipper** 名ジッパー, ファスナー
- □ **zippered** 形ジッパー付きの

E-CAT

English **C**onversational **A**bility **T**est
国際英語会話能力検定

● E-CATとは…
英語が話せるようになるためのテストです。インターネットベースで、30分であなたの発話力をチェックします。

www.ecatexam.com

iTEP

Academic · Business · SLATE
International Test of English Proficiency

● iTEP®とは…
世界各国の企業、政府機関、アメリカの大学300校以上が、英語能力判定テストとして採用。オンラインによる90分のテストで文法、リーディング、リスニング、ライティング、スピーキングの5技能をスコア化。iTEP®は、留学、就職、海外赴任などに必要な、世界に通用する英語力を総合的に評価する画期的なテストです。

www.itepexamjapan.com

ラダーシリーズ
Jon's Chopsticks ガイコク人ニッポン体験記

2012年2月2日　第1刷発行
2020年4月7日　第5刷発行

著　者　レベッカ・ミルナー

発行者　浦　晋亮

発行所　IBCパブリッシング株式会社
　　　　〒162-0804 東京都新宿区中里町29番3号
　　　　菱秀神楽坂ビル9F
　　　　Tel. 03-3513-4511　Fax. 03-3513-4512
　　　　www.ibcpub.co.jp

© IBC Publishing, Inc. 2012

印刷　株式会社シナノパブリッシングプレス
装丁　伊藤 理恵　　本文イラスト　結城麗
組版データ　Optima LTD Standard Roman + Imprint MT Shadow Regular

落丁本・乱丁本は、小社宛にお送りください。送料小社負担にてお取り替えいたします。本書の無断複写（コピー）は著作権法上での例外を除き禁じられています。

Printed in Japan
ISBN978-4-7946-0126-1